KEEPING
MR. RIGHT

KEEPING MR. RIGHT

The Gay Man's Guide to Lasting Relationships

DR. KENNETH D. GEORGE

alyson books
los angeles

MANUFACTURED IN THE UNITED STATES OF AMERICA.

THIS TRADE PAPERBACK ORIGINAL IS PUBLISHED BY ALYSON PUBLICATIONS,
P.O. BOX 4371, LOS ANGELES, CALIFORNIA 90078-4371.
DISTRIBUTION IN THE UNITED KINGDOM BY TURNAROUND PUBLISHER SERVICES LTD.,
UNIT 3, OLYMPIA TRADING ESTATE, COBURG ROAD, WOOD GREEN,
LONDON N22 6TZ ENGLAND.

FIRST EDITION: JUNE 2004

04 05 06 07 08 a 10 9 8 7 6 5 4 3 2 1

ISBN 1-55583-800-6

LIBRARY OF CONGRESS CATALOGING-IN-PUBLICATION DATA
  GEORGE, KENNETH D., DR.
    KEEPING MR. RIGHT : THE GAY MAN'S GUIDE TO HEALTHY
  RELATIONSHIPS / KENNETH D. GEORGE—1ST ED.
    ISBN 1-55583-800-6
  1. GAY COUPLES. 2. GAY MEN. 3. INTERPERSONAL RELATIONS. I. TITLE.
  HQ76.25.G46 2004
  306.76'62—DC22   2004043672

CREDITS
COVER PHOTOGRAPHY BY DALE DURFEE/STONE COLLECTION/GETTY IMAGES.
COVER DESIGN BY MATT SAMS.

To Christopher S. Beck,
My Spouse

It is a great to know I have Christopher to come home to. He allows me to yell and scream when I have had a frustrating day. He is comfortable enough with me that I can cry when I want to cry. He has taught me to admit when I am wrong and to say, "I'm sorry." He would never do anything to ever intentionally hurt me. He is there for me—whether it be a "good morning," a welcome home kiss, or to pull the covers over me when I go to bed. But most of all I love him because he sings, dances, and makes me laugh, and I love him more today than when we made a commitment to spend our lives together. Throughout our years of growing older together, Christopher has always been just as sweet, kind, playful, passionate, cute, and sexy as the day I met him. We have a relationship in which we play together and laugh with each other and at each other. He has made my life a fun-filled adventure. He is my friend, playmate, lover, spouse, and life partner. His commitment to our relationship and me is shown in so many different ways. I like that Christopher and I are a successful male couple.

Contents

ACKNOWLEDGMENTS

Attempting to acknowledge all of those who have helped make this book possible is almost an impossible task.

I cannot fully express my thanks and gratitude to the hundreds of male couples who contributed their life stories to this book. And a special thank you to one of the most successful male couple I have ever met, our friends and neighbors George and Louis, who met when they were 16 and are soon to celebrate their 25th anniversary—their love for each other is an inspiration to all of us.

I would like to acknowledge and thank our neighbors. Many of these men and women had never before been friends with a male couple. These neighbors have been very supportive ever since Christopher and I moved to Florida. And a big thank you to my many "sewing buddies," to name just a few: Kerstin, Susie, Sandy, Cathy, Kassy, Hermie, Gerri, Linda, Joyce, Anne, Dianne, Alice, Gavin, and Bob. I also appreciate all the support I received from Jeff, Ken, Jim, Lisa, Francesca, Janice, and Nancy.

I owe enormous thanks to my editor, Nick Street, and his editor in training, Whitney Friedlander, at Alyson Publications for their valuable help in the final editing of the manuscript. Most of all, I want to thank two extra-special men who have been my friends for many years, Robert Ewe and Andrew Behrendt.

Chapter One
The Basics:
Successful Male
Couples

After *Mr. Right Is Out There: The Gay Man's Guide to Finding and Maintaining Love* was published, I began receiving e-mail messages from many other gay men in all parts of North America, Europe, Australia, Asia, South America, as well as some remote places I had never heard about. These men told me so much about their relationships, most of which began the usual way: Two men found themselves attracted to each other, talked, went out on a date (having sex sometime soon after meeting—some on the day they met), then another date, and a few more dates. They eventually "fell in love" (without really knowing too much about each other), called themselves a couple, and moved in with each other.

Some of the men who wrote have developed and maintained successful relationships; they are "living happily ever after."

"Wow, what a great book you wrote! We were at the bookstore looking for a gift for a friend. We saw the title of your book and it really was exactly what we were looking for. Of course, when we got home we read it before wrapping it. We enjoyed reading about other men who have stayed a couple, and the book also gave us some great ideas. We are both in our mid 30s, have been a couple for almost 10 years, and have our own floral business together. We also have many other similar interests, still attracted to each other, and we like each other. We loved your description of male couples as best friends. That's us. Thanks for writing a great book and for a perfect gift for our friend."

However, for many of the other men who wrote, this just didn't happen. The two men started to argue, fought with each other, didn't get along, and didn't take the time to become good friends. Some of these unsuccessful relationships lasted for months, others for years, but eventually the two men separated. These men needed to learn how to develop and maintain a successful relationship as a male couple. Following are some excerpts from their e-mail messages:

• "My boyfriend, whom I love more than anyone I've ever been in love with, recently told me he needs more space. We have been seeing each other for 10 months. What should I do?"

• "The first six months of our relationship were wonderful, but now he is gradually beginning to pull away from me."

• "He told me he loved me. He said he wanted to spend the rest of his life with me and he would never stop loving me. We both spoke often about our future. But after six months together he started cruising and having sex with other men."

• "After four years he told me he wasn't in love with me anymore. He said he wanted his independence back and suggested we start dating others."

• "I love him very much, and I know he loves me. But we just couldn't get along with each other. We stopped seeing each other almost three months ago."

• "After three years together, I have started asking myself if I'm wasting my time or if I should hang in there."

• "Being a therapist with a degree in psychology, I believe I should be well-grounded and suited to finding Mr. Right. But three boyfriends in the last seven years has disproved that assumption."

• "I lived with my lover for three years, and we were together for a total of six years. We broke up two years ago. He had an affair and told me about it, which really hurt me. We aren't together any longer."

• "I split with my last lover about two years ago. Men are all the same. All they do is disagree. We never agreed on much. We were constantly fighting. But I'm ready to be a couple again."

• "I just finished reading your book *Mr. Right Is Out There,* and thoroughly enjoyed it. I had been in a relationship for three years that has recently ended. We love each other—we still do. But all we did was argue. The constant bickering got to both of us."

• "I have had two short-term relationships, one for four months and the other for a year. I do want to find someone to have a long-term relationship, and I do need to learn how to do it right."

• "I have never stayed in a relationship longer than two years in my whole life (except for the time when I was with my first lover from the age of 18 to about 28). I'm 45 now."

• "I love him so much. We dated for six months and lived together for 3½ years. I love spending time with him. He's funny, he's good looking, he's smart, and he makes me laugh. I can't imagine my life without him. He is my first real boyfriend. I want to be with him always, but we keep arguing over and over about the same things. We are both tired of these fights."

• "He doesn't love me any more. And anyway, he clearly has serious problems. How could I possibly fix him? He is so messed up, and I'm no shrink. I want out!"

• "I have had nothing but short-lived relationships. I'm the one who always gets dumped."

• "I often find myself depressed, because in the 12 years I've been out I've never had a relationship last longer than eight months."

WHAT DO GAY MEN SAY ABOUT THEIR RELATIONSHIPS?

Why is it that some of the relationships between two men become successful and others become unsuccessful? Since the publication of *Mr. Right Is Out There: The Gay Man's Guide to Finding and Maintaining Love*, Christopher and I have tried to answer that question. We have been in contact with hundreds of gay men and male couples. We have visited with some of these men in the United States, England, Australia, South America, and Asia and have communicated by e-mail, phone, and letters with many others. We asked the men who were:

• **single:** "Why do you want to become a couple?"
• **presently single, but who had been in three or more relationships:** "What were the characteristics of your relationships?"
• **dating for a few months and were talking about becoming a couple:** "What do you think are the characteristics of a successful male couple?"
• **a couple for more than five years:** "Do you consider your relationship a success—and if so—what makes it so?"

1. The two most common reasons given by single men for becoming a male couple were sex and loneliness.

> Erik: "I'm tired of tricking, sex with different men, and not just having one man. To tell the truth, it sounds great having lots of sex partners, but I really want to have sex with just one man."
>
> Kurt: "I have friends over once or twice a week, sometimes more, and I have a fuck buddy, but I'm lonely. I want a lover to have dinner with, watch TV with, and go out with. I'm really tired of doing so many things by myself."

2. The men who had difficulty maintaining a relationship identified the following as being typical of their relationships:

- They lacked respect for each other.
- They expressed lots of anger.
- They had frequent arguments.
- Conflicts were rarely resolved.
- They were emotionally and physically abusive to each other.
- Each engaged in emotional withdrawal or silent treatment; neither was there for the other.
- Each lacked trust in his lover and in the relationship.
- They didn't accept each other's needs.
- They didn't really like each other.
- Each blamed the other for things that went wrong in the relationship.
- Each complained to friends about his lover's behavior, saying negative things about him and the relationship.
- They lacked communication and didn't share their feelings with each other.
- Each tried to change the other.
- They criticized each other.
- They spent little time together.
- Both felt lonely or neglected.
- Sexual desire and activity decreased.
- Each had sex with others.

• Decisions were made without any regard for the wishes of the other or for the relationship.
• They had few shared interests.
• There was not much affection between them.

The men who were just beginning their relationships believed the following were characteristics of a successful male couple (with my comments in parentheses):

• **long-lasting** (Being successful isn't just long-lasting.)
• **quality time together** (Quality is extremely important, but quantity is important too. Five minutes a day of quality time is not enough. Relationships need more time than that. Couples need to do things together that they both enjoy, and they need to have fun together. They should also do the chores together—setting the table, cooking dinner, and putting the dishes away. Couples should have some common interests and spend quality time doing those things together.)
• **best friends** (Your lover needs to be your best friend—period, end of statement. He is number 1—not your mother, your other friends, or your dog. There should be no one who is a better friend to you than your lover.)
• **trust** (This is the "heart" of a successful relationship between two men. We don't have a marriage certificate or laws to protect our rights as a couple, and we frequently lack the support of our families; trust is knowing our lover will be there. Through this trust, we are willing to take the time and energy to work on this relationship and to have it grow and become successful.)
• **good sex** (Lots of sex—as determined by the two of you, not what surveys have determined or what other gay men call the "norm.")
• **lots of affection** (Demonstrating your love for each other and being playful together.)
• **respect each other** (Your lover is just as important as you are and should be treated with the same respect that you treat yourself—but, of course, you have to love and respect yourself

before you can respect and love someone else. You can read more on this topic in *Mr. Right Is Out There*.)

• **unconditional love** (There is no such thing. If your lover says you must love him unconditionally, he really is saying to you "I don't want to change." Male couples need to change in order to meet each other's expectations.)

• **equality** (I don't think this is possible in a relationship between two men—but more on that topic in Chapter Six.)

• **intimacy** (You share your deepest hurts, dreams, desires, fears, and fantasies with each other. You can read more on this topic in *Mr. Right Is Out There*.)

• **commitment** (The agreement you both make to each other to do the work needed to make the relationship successful. With commitment you never say, "I'm out of here," or "You can leave if you don't like it.")

• **communication** (Communication is essential to a successful relationship.)

• **few arguments** (All couples have conflicts, but the methods of resolving the conflicts differ between couples. Some couples have volatile arguments, and others avoid conflicts; successful couples, however, take the time to find out what is really going on between the two of them to cause the disagreement.)

• **fun** (A couple that has fun together, stays together.)

The men who had been together for more than five years and considered their relationship a success told us:

• "My lover is my best friend, and I like him; I have made him first in my life over my work, over TV, over everything. I make time in my life for him every single day."

• "My lover and I have made a commitment to each other; of course we have disagreements, but I never considered leaving him. We work it out. I feel totally accepted, respected, and supported by him. We don't criticize each other; we talk about what we can do differently."

• "I have fun with my lover; we laugh and touch; we confide; we agree on values, goals, and sex. We look for the good in each other. We have similar interests, but we try new things."

• "We decided at the beginning of our relationship to be monogamous. It's been a struggle but well worth the effort. We have put all of our sexual energy into our relationship."

• "We respect each other's wishes and know we can't always have our way; we have disagreements. Decisions are made fairly, some together, some by me, and some by him. We both make changes when needed."

• "We trust each other; we are honest; I tell him what I'm feeling. I love the closeness; we share with each other. We listen to the other."

• "We are equally dependent on each other, and we are equally independent from each other. We do so much together and agree on most issues, but we have a clear sense of self and do things by ourselves. Clearly, we think for ourselves."

• "We love our time together; we talk a lot with each other about the little and the big things. We have many memories of the things we did together and frequently remind each other of those times."

In talking with successful male couples who had been together for more than five years, Christopher and I observed that in their relationships they:

• took the time to communicate
• listened to each other
• had fun together
• continued to be sexual with each other rather than with others
• resolved conflicts fairly
• had similar goals
• made changes when necessary

Felix (and Jon): "We are kind to each other. We accept each other as not being perfect. We are both willing to make changes for the other (it was OK not going to the annual gay dance when Jon had the flu). We never think of getting out of our relationship even after we have had a big argument."

Bill (and Alex): "We've been through many crises together. Alex was there when I learned I was infected with HIV. He has been more than a lover, he has been my best friend—a friend that has stayed closer than any family member. He was my knight in shining armor when I met him and he has proved to be so throughout our 15 years together."

From these couples we have learned that **a successful relationship is one where the two men continue (1) to love each other; (2) to be best friends; (3) to be attracted to each other; and (4) to have sex with each other.**

SUCCESSFUL MALE COUPLES

When we were boys we had fantasies about the men we saw on television and in the movies—we would meet one of these men, fall in love, love would lead to "marriage," and "marriage" meant living with him "happily ever after." As a gay man, this theme is the same—we meet another man, date, have sex, fall in love, decide to become a couple, and live happily ever after. But the truth is that for some men living happily ever after doesn't happen because they became a couple for the wrong reasons, such as:

• **Happiness:** Happiness can not be based on having a lover. Once you say "I need a lover to be happy" or "I need a new lover to be happy," you have set yourself up for relationship problems.

George: "I will spend the rest of my life with Erik and will always be happy."

Martin: "I'm so much happier now that I have Bob."

• **Love:** A major problem for most relationships is the myth that "love" is the "magic" ingredient and that maintaining our love for each other is the key to having a successful relationship.

Stuart: "We are so much in love. We only have eyes for each other."

• **Sex:** After a couple years together, the lust between the two men begins to decline. There is always something more exciting about a new boyfriend—lovers get older, set in their ways, and not as sexually exciting as a new one.

John: "We just met and we are already in love."

Pete: "I could tell the moment I saw him that he was Mr. Right."

• **Loneliness:** Being alone is different than being lonely. Feeling lonely when you are single could mean that you don't like yourself well enough to see that you are an exciting, fun, and enjoyable person. If you don't see that, a lover won't see you as an exciting, fun, and enjoyable person.

Sid: "I'm always lonely until I find a lover."

Noel: "It's so painful to me to be alone, I always had a lover."

Creating a successful relationship means more than being happy with him, being in love, and having great sex. These reasons are a setup for an unsuccessful relationship because you don't see those danger signs that tell you he is really Mr. Wrong. For many of us, being in these short-lived relationships with Mr. Wrong (unless we've already found another boyfriend) has become very frustrating, discouraging, and painful. We lose the most important man in our life. We feel awful. We become angry. The breakup can overwhelm us with scary changes, decisions we must now make, new responsibilities, questions about "What do I want to do now?" and fears about going back out into the "marketplace." The problems with our lover may have begun a long time before the breakup, but the hurt often lasts for months afterwards. Some of us even begin to think staying single would be better than going through the dating process again with the possibility of another breakup.

If breaking up is so awful, why do we keep looking for Mr.

Right and continue getting into relationships over and over again? Because it feels so good to be in love and to have a lover who:

- loves us
- is supportive
- is understanding
- knows our thoughts and feelings
- knows the real us
- meets our needs
- accepts us

And most of all, having a lover is a lot more fun than being single. We also believe this time we have really found Mr. Right and this relationship will be the one that is successful because we've had more experience!

But after another breakup, you may even begin to believe successful relationships are the exception rather than the norm—but that just isn't true. **Many male couples do become successful.**

Our neighbors George and Louis met when both were 16 and in high school. They are still together 24 years later. Christopher and I have been together for 17 years, and most of our friends are male couples that have been together for 10 years or more. The men in these successful relationships are supportive, accept each other's differences, are playful, communicate, are honest, trust each other, are monogamous, and have grown together both independently and as a couple. These men are best friends.

According to census figures released in 2001, there were 601,209 same-sex couples living in the United States. (Since many gay men and lesbians are closeted and were not honest in completing the census form, I estimate that there are many more same-sex couples.) Many of these couples are successful.

Do You Have a Successful Relationship?

A yes answer to most of the following questions indicates you are in a successful relationship:

• Can you identify what you admire about your lover?
• Does he accept that you have other friends?
• Is he proud of your accomplishments?
• Does he ask for and respect your opinions?
• Does he see you as an intelligent adult whose opinion he respects?
• Do you know you will not be put down as "stupid" or "crazy" when your views are different from his?
• Can your opinion be different than his when you are with friends?
• Does he respect your right to make decisions that affect your own life?
• Do you know that when you make mistakes, he will be at your side—believing in you and your abilities?
• Does he listen to you?
• Does he talk about his feelings?
• Does he have any other interests besides you?
• Does he take responsibility for his actions and not blame you for his failures?
• Are you trusted to use your time as you see fit, without feeling as if you have to account for your whereabouts every moment?
• Are you confident your relationship can weather a major disagreement?
• Can you be yourself with him, knowing that he likes you as you truly are?
• Are you and your lover friends? Best friends?

Successful relationships are those in which both men do the work to develop and maintain the relationship as best friends: valuing and respecting each other, accepting each other's differences. This means accepting each other's goodness, craziness, weirdness, weaknesses, strengths, faults, happy side, and sad side—and both knowing and fulfilling the expectations of the other. This book is about attaining this goal—having a successful relationship with another man.

So What Do You Have to Do in Order to Have A Successful Relationship?

1. Choose Mr. Right.

It's interesting that arranged heterosexual relationships are usually successful in cultures where the parents or a matchmaker selects the man and woman for each other. Now I have never heard of an arranged "marriage" between two men, but—it could work. Certainly being in love doesn't always guarantee the relationship will be successful.

A fairly good guarantee for an unsuccessful relationship is to choose a lover only because he is handsome and young-looking, with a cute smile, a nice butt, beautiful hair, and a great build. A fairly good guarantee for a successful relationship is to choose a lover who has all the characteristics you would want in a best friend. In a successful relationship, your lover is your best friend— you can rely on him and you look forward to seeing and being with him. Choosing the right lover is more important than choosing the right car (at least for most of us), however, many of us spend more time researching the best car than we do researching the best man for us.

2. Realize that most of what you believe about relationships are myths.

First of all, there is the myth that we are going to spend a lifetime with Mr. Right and not have any conflicts. I can guarantee you there will be disagreements over finances, family, friends, sex, and leisure activities. No relationship is safe from disagreements. However, encountering problems in a relationship is no reason to remain single, to have an unhappy relationship, or to keep getting out of relationships.

And the second most common myth—that gay men are incapable of forming lasting relationships, and most male couples are "doomed to fail"—has destroyed the relationships of many male couples. When the men believe it and when conflicts begin, rather than stay in the relationship and work on it they end their relationship. It's very important to remind yourself that male couples are just as successful as heterosexual couples.

Other myths about relationships include:

- The passion between the two lovers must be intense and ever-present.
- Both men are always happy.
- Satisfactions should come from your lover.
- Relationships will cure loneliness.
- Lovers must tell each other everything.
- Lovers agree on every issue.
- Arguments are never volatile.
- Monogamy does not exist, or is not possible between two men.
- Good sex means a good relationship.
- The two men never dislike each other.
- Sex will take care of itself.
- Relationships don't require work.
- Relationships never change.

3. **Take a good look at yourself.**

I urge you to consider the following questions:

- Am I sure the problems in my relationships have not been caused by me? If they are, what am I doing to cause them?
- Do the same problems occur again with a new lover?
- Am I reasonably sure I can and will select Mr. Right the next time? Or will I be attracted to another Mr. Wrong?
- Am I willing to make some changes in myself?
- What do I need to do differently in order to make my relationships successful?

The emphasis in these questions is on you—**you** need to do something differently in order for **you** to have a better relationship. It means it is **you** who brought **you** to where **you** are and it is **you** who can change **your** relationships into what **you** would like them to be.

4. Work on your relationship.

Men in successful relationships make the necessary changes in their behavior to develop and maintain a successful relationship with each other. However, if you don't think you can make any changes and you believe "This is who I am," or "I have always been this way," or "You can't teach an old dog new tricks," then you're making excuses for not changing. If you believe you're helpless in changing yourself in order to have a successful relationship, then reading this book is going to be a waste of time.

Making these changes, however, takes work. But developing and maintaining a successful relationship really takes work. Some of the changes are easy to make, but they will tell your lover you are there for him, such as:

- expressing your love with daily hugs and expressions of appreciation
- greeting your lover when he arrives home
- listening to his stories
- celebrating his successes
- turning off the TV, leaving the dirty dishes in the sink, and just sitting with your arms around each other (Even if it means a dirty kitchen, isn't sitting with him more important?)
- going out for a romantic candlelit dinner for two
- communicating with each other every day, even for just a few minutes

You spend time washing and waxing your car, cleaning your home, and mowing your lawn, but how much time do you spend working on your relationship? While we're pursuing our career, most of us overlook how important our lover is to us. During the first few years, our relationship is fueled by intense lust. But after those first few years as a couple, when was the last take time you and your lover went out for a romantic dinner—just the two of you? The last time you hugged or kissed your lover other than while having sex? The last time you talked without the television being on? The last time you bought him a gift for no reason?

How often have you shown your lover how much you love him?

Think about your dog and how much time he or she spends demonstrating his or her love for you:

- Your dog is always so pleased and excited to see you.
- Your dog runs up and gives you a great big kiss when you get home.

If you're now thinking, *I expect this from my dog, but I don't expect this from my lover, and I certainly hope he doesn't expect this from me*, ask yourself, *Why not?* How much time does it take to show him you are pleased and excited to see him and to give him a great big kiss? Two minutes! Even if you go in and out of your house three times a day, this would only take six minutes.

Christopher and I own three dogs, and when we come home they get so excited, even if we've been gone only an hour. And sometimes Kahli (the Dachshund) gets so excited she pees on the floor. Their greetings, however, help to make our family a family.

But even more importantly, when either one of us comes home, we always greet each other with a hug and a kiss. I think we learned the importance of greeting each other from our dogs. It seems odd that dogs know more about relationships than most men.

Activities

1. Plan a new way to greet your lover.
   - The one at home rushes to greet his lover who has just arrived home.
   - The one arriving home rushes to find his lover.
   - You greet each other with enthusiasm, excitement, and a smile. Say "Hello," "I love you," and "I'm so glad to see you." Give each other a hug and a passionate kiss. Then ask each other, "How was your day?" and listen to the answer.

2. Schedule 15 minutes with your lover. During this time tell him all the reasons you love him and all the cute things he does that make him special.

3. Smile whenever you see your lover. If you already smile a lot, perhaps you will now be smiling even more.

4. At least six times a day touch your lover and look him in the eye and say something nice.

5. Make a request for support from your lover. Your lover can honor or refuse your request however his decision cannot be discussed, negotiated, or argued.

These activities have helped you look at yourself and at your relationship and to make some changes. Did you have trouble doing any of them? If you didn't do an activity, identify the reasons for this decision. How did you feel after doing each activity? If he said no to your request for support, how would you change your request so he would say "yes?" Would you have trouble doing any of these activities again? Is your relationship worth the time it took?

Most of us who have had unsuccessful relationships are eager to work on our current relationship—and for good reasons. Being in a successful relationship is fantastic! **A basic premises of this book is that (1) you can change what you want to change and (2) you are responsible for making your own relationships successful.**

6. **Read this book.**

In talking with gay men from all different places, Christopher and I were amazed at how some of the issues that helped many men also prevented others from having successful relationships. These men talked about how these topics affected their relationships and how they resolved those issues. But most of all, these men reaffirmed what we already knew: Most gay men want to be in a successful relationship.

Unfortunately, most of these men (and I really believe most people) are not prepared to have a relationship. They believe all they have to do is meet a man, fall in love, and call themselves a couple. **But the truth is that relationships require more than our love for each other, we must learn how to make them successful.**

How can we learn to make our relationships successful? Before the publication of *Mr. Right Is Out There*, we were never given a male couple instruction manual, nor have we been taught how to maintain and repair our relationships, and we don't have someone to talk with about our relationships. When things go wrong, we frequently don't know what is wrong, what to say, or how to change the relationship. There are very few male couple role models visible to us to observe or to give us advice. Given all of this, it's no wonder we walk away when the relationship starts to break down and our anger flares.

Each of us has done the work to learn how to become successful in our career, drive a car, do well in our hobbies, to win at computer and card games, as well as to read and balance a checkbook. But very few of us have ever done the work to learn how to make our relationships successful. This book will help you to do just that.

There is no magic pill for developing and maintaining a successful relationship, and there is no miracle. If you bought this book in the hope it will *help* you to have a successful relationship, you are in luck. **This is a book for those gay men and male couples who want to make the changes they need to make to have a successful relationship**. After you have decided to make changes, I recommend that you then change your goal from "I want to be in a relationship" to "I want to be in a successful relationship." This is an attainable goal.

Reading this book will help you to attain that goal. You will be doing various activities as well as looking at different male couples who had to make changes in order to develop and maintain a successful relationship. In particular, you will be looking at the following men and their relationships:

- Ryan and Ethan have been a couple for 10 years, and there is a 15-year age difference between the two of them. They met in a gay bar one evening, started dating, and became a couple. Ethan is a salesman at a large department store and hopes someday to become a buyer. He enjoys working out in the gym and being cruised by other men. Ryan is a reporter, enjoys his work, loves his home, and was so happy to have met Ethan and to finally become a couple. None of their friends gave this relationship any chance of succeeding.

• Jeff and Gary are both 75 years old and have been a couple for 50 years. They are both now retired and live in Los Angeles, but they met in San Francisco while they were in the Navy. I met them at a gay bookstore in West Hollywood while giving a talk about *Mr. Right Is Out There*. They e-mailed me several times about how much they enjoyed my talk and my book, and they shared a lot about their relationship. I really enjoyed their e-mail messages and learned a lot about their relationship, especially during the 1950s. They are both homophobic, but growing up in that era it is understandable. A year after I met them, they invited Christopher and me to their 50th anniversary party. We spent three days in their home, met their friends, and had a great time.

• Glen and Mike are both 35 years old and have been together for eight years. Glen designs computer programs for a large corporation and Mike works as a legal secretary in a law firm. They met through mutual nongay friends. Shortly after meeting, they moved in together in the same small city in the Midwest where they were both born and met. They both enjoy living near their respective families.

• Ricky and Shawn met 15 years ago on a gay cruise to the Caribbean. They met at the pool, liked each other, and spent most of the cruise having sex and making plans to be together after the cruise ended. They knew the major problem for the two of them would be the miles that separated them. Ricky was a physician in private practice in Boston when they met, and Shawn was a teacher living in Chicago.

• Lance is a lawyer and Al is an interior designer. They live in

Minneapolis and have now been a couple for 12 years. When they met they were members of the same church. Their relationship began one Sunday morning when they stayed for the social hour and started talking with each other about their interests and being "unmarried." They then went out to brunch together and made plans to meet the following Sunday at church. Lance, however, decided to call Monday evening and asked Al out to dinner. They had dinner together that evening as well as every night that week. They went to church together the next Sunday and have been together ever since.

• One day while waiting to check out at the grocery store, Philip started talking with Jose, who was in the line behind him. They discovered they lived in the same apartment building, so Philip waited for Jose, and they walked home together. They made plans to meet later that evening for dinner, and they moved in together six months later. This relationship never became successful, however.

• George and Louis met when they were both 16 and in high school. They called themselves "best friends" from the very beginning and soon identified themselves as "lovers." They finished high school, went to college together, and both began working. They bought their first home and have included both their families in their lives. Christopher and I met George and Louis six years ago while they were in Florida looking for property to buy in order to build a second home. They were looking at the property next to ours, and we started talking. We both knew instantly that we were male couples because they wore matching rings as Christopher and I did. George and Louis are the first couple (gay or nongay) that I have ever met who were teenage lovers and will soon be celebrating their 25th anniversary.

• Christopher and I are both "only children" and coincidentally were born in the same Chicago suburb (but not in the same year—I'm 20 years older than Christopher). We met in Philadelphia at a fund-raiser for a gay organization, dated, decided to become a couple, and years later had a commitment ceremony. Christopher has continued his work as an artist, and I'm now an emeritus professor, having retired from the University of Pennsylvania after the publication of *Mr. Right Is Out There*. We have left Philadelphia and are now living full-time in southern Florida. At the time this book is published we will have celebrated 17 years together, and we continue to do the work to maintain a successful relationship.

All of these men believe the work required to become a successful male couple is well worth doing. They have all met their Mr. Right, become best friends, and are living happily together. The kind of relationship these couples have developed and maintained is the same kind most of us dream to have.

The chapters that follow include the work you need to do to make those changes in order to develop and maintain a successful relationship with your Mr. Right. Some of the changes you will need to make are easy, such as saying "I" instead of "you," and some of the changes are more difficult, such as accepting Mr. Right's differences.

Chapter Two: Becoming a successful couple means behaving like Mr. Right rather than behaving like Mr. Wrong.

Chapter Three: Becoming a successful couple means accepting Mr. Right and negotiating some changes rather than living with annoying differences.

Chapter Four: Becoming a successful couple means knowing what you can expect from Mr. Right rather than having a relationship without a job description.

Chapter Five: Becoming a successful couple means resolving what's going on when you have disagreements and arguments rather then ending the relationship.

Chapter Six: Becoming a successful couple means treating your lover as your best friend rather than trying to control him.

Chapter Seven: Becoming a successful couple means continuing to have an exciting sex life with each other rather than with others.

Chapter Eight: Becoming a successful couple means continuing the work on your changing relationship rather than saying, "I'm out of here."

Chapter Two
Start Behaving
as Mr. Right

Most of us at one time or another meet a man that we really like, we date, and we fall in love, finally calling ourselves a couple. We start making plans for our life together. Both of us are happy and enjoy being together.

Ricky and Shawn met 15 years ago on a gay cruise to the Caribbean. They met at the pool, liked each other, and spent most of the cruise having sex and making plans to be together after the cruise ended. They knew the major problem for the two of them would be the miles that separated them. Ricky was a physician in private practice in Boston when they met, and Shawn was a teacher living in Chicago. After docking, they continued the relationship by talking on the phone almost every day. They spent long weekends together in Chicago, and Shawn spent his next summer vacation in Boston with Ricky.

One day while waiting to check out at the grocery store, Philip started talking with Jose, who was in the line behind him. They discovered they lived in the same apartment building, so Philip waited for Jose, and they walked home together. They made plans to meet later that evening for dinner. Jose was a graduate student from Spain attending the local university, and Philip was an executive at a major bank. They were attracted to each other, liked each other, and started seeing each other almost every evening. Six months later they moved in together.

STOP BEHAVING LIKE MR. WRONG

Being a couple feels great, but many times after meeting Mr. Right and becoming a couple, something goes wrong—we start to disagree with each other and we get annoyed with some of the things the other does. We have arguments, and we say things that really hurt. We get angry and don't speak to each other for days. We even call our friends and confide, "He's such a bitch. I don't know what I ever saw in him." And their response, "I'm so sorry, but you know what they say about gay relationships? They just don't work." And eventually the relationship ends. But it doesn't have to be that way.

Most of what goes wrong in our relationship has nothing to do with being gay—it has everything to do with being a man. Many of us may think we are different from nongay men, and in some ways that may be true. But all of us—gay and nongay—were boys at one time, and we learned from our parents, peers, teachers, and the media how we were suppose to behave. For example, most of us learned:

1. to be in **control** (we learned how to get our way).

For the first few months Ricky would fly to Chicago and would spend long weekends with Shawn. A typical discussion during these visits went something like this:

Ricky: "But of course you will move to Boston. I'm in private practice and make more money than you do. It wouldn't make any sense for me to move to Chicago."

Shawn: "I don't think I can afford to move to Boston, I love my job, and I really don't want to leave my friends or leave Chicago."

Ricky: "I will take care of the moving expenses, and I have lots of friends who can help you find a teaching position in Boston."

2. not to show our **feelings**, except **anger.**

Jose: "Let's go to New Orleans for Thanksgiving."

Philip: "We can't. I always spend Thanksgiving with my aunt and uncle."

Jose: "But times have changed. You have me now, and we should go to New Orleans before I have to return to Spain."

Philip: "We can't go to New Orleans. My aunt and uncle are expecting us."

Jose: "I really am pissed that you want to spend this time with your relatives rather than in New Orleans."

Philip: "You have such a nasty attitude."

Jose: "Screw you! Go visit your precious family. I'll go to New Orleans by myself."

3. to **fight** to win.

Shawn: "Why does it have to be your way? My teaching job is important to me, and my friends are also important. I'm not going to leave Chicago and move to Boston."

Ricky: "I don't intend to leave a lucrative private practice and move to Chicago. All of my friends agree it would be stupid for me to leave Boston. This relationship isn't going anywhere."

Most of us do know that hiding our feelings, fighting to win, wanting to be in control, and getting angry are not good for us— these behaviors cause ulcers, heart attacks, early deaths, and also have an impact on our relationships. But not all of us know that these same behaviors have a greater effect on male couples than they do on nongay couples. These behaviors have caused many of us to have far too many unsuccessful relationships because both of us are behaving the way we believe men are suppose to behave, and **this behavior is the behavior of Mr. Wrong.**

How do we communicate with a man who is uncomfortable sharing his feelings? How can we continue to love a man who constantly disagrees with us? How will the two of us make decisions? How will we resolve our differences? It's no wonder that:

- We have arguments over "who is going to do the dishes tonight" or "what program we will watch on television" or "which one of us did that cute boy flirt with."
- Our love for each other withers and dies when the two of us become consumed with anger, have conflicts, disagreements, arguments, and always fight to win.
- So many of us have difficulty forming and maintaining a successful relationship with another man who also wants to be in control, doesn't communicate or show his feelings, and who fights to be right.
- We don't stay in a relationship for very long.
- So many of the men we date soon begin to behave like Mr. Wrong.

When Christopher and I started living together, I had been a professor for years and I "knew" how to get what I wanted. The tone of voice I used (which I was unaware of) sounded very demanding, and when Christopher heard that tone he reacted very negatively and told me I was "ordering" him as I would have ordered one of my students. Of course I denied it! When I finally realized this was a problem in our relationship, I had to learn to hear the tone of voice I was using, then not to use that demanding tone, and finally how to request what I wanted rather than demand it. I had to learn to be Mr. Right and to stop being the man I had learned to become over the years.

Most of us have learned how to behave like a man—to behave like Mr. Wrong—but very few of us have ever learned how to behave like Mr. Right.

LEARNING TO BE MR. RIGHT

Men who form successful relationships have learned how to be Mr. Right. They:

- communicate freely with their lover about the things that are important to them
- know they can think, feel, believe, and behave differently from their lover without fearing the relationship will end
- have disagreements, but don't fight in a way that makes their lover feel bad
- get angry, but don't react in ways that harm the relationship or hurt their lover
- express their feelings
- don't feel threatened when their lover says no

Many men wrongly believe we "just sort of know" how to be Mr. Right, but that just isn't true. We have to learn how to become Mr. Right. However, there are no schools that teach us how to be Mr. Right, and even if there were, there are very few qualified teachers; therefore most of us learn to be Mr. Right by watching other men, male couples, and by trial and error. No wonder there are so many failed relationships!

The very first step in developing and maintaining a successful relationship is to learn how to be Mr. Right. Many of us have dated a man we thought was our Mr. Right only to discover he was cold and distant, controlling, argumentative, and never wrong. And the men who dated us may have thought we were their Mr. Right, but we also became their Mr. Wrong. In order to be Mr. Right, we have to learn how to:

- express our feelings by saying "I" rather than "you"

- listen to our lover
- respond to our lover with empathy
- not interpret his behavior
- fight fairly
- treat our lover as our best friend

Very few of us have ever learned how to be Mr. Right. But you can start right now!

MEN IN SUCCESSFUL RELATIONSHIPS SHOW AND EXPRESS THEIR FEELINGS

It is important that you learn to use your feelings—feelings tell you what is going on with you and in your relationship.

- Are you comfortable showing or expressing your feelings to your lover?
- Would your friends say you are comfortable showing or expressing your feelings?
- What feelings are difficult for you to express?
- What feelings are easy for you to express?
- Can you open up to your lover?
- Are you emotionally available to your lover?
- Do you know what your lover is feeling?
- Does your lover show or express his feelings with you?

However, feelings have gotten a bad reputation with most men. This started for us when we were boys and began our "lessons" on becoming a man. As boys we heard our fathers say "Don't be a scaredy-cat" or "Boys shouldn't be frightened" when we were scared. And everyone told us "Big boys don't cry," so we thought something was wrong with us because we were frightened and we did cry. We were also told to be "the man of the house" and to be strong, so we learned to not acknowledge our weaknesses. We may have even been ridiculed for showing tenderness, empathy, and sensitivity. How often did you see your father show affection? Remember the time you were going to kiss your father and he shook your hand instead? We were frequently told not to let our feelings "get in the way" or to "keep a stiff upper lip."

Activity

As a boy, you may not have been able to experience or express your feelings in ways that were different from your family. Observe your family today (especially your father) and observe how they (he) experience or express their (his) feelings. How different are you from them (him)?

As we got older, we continued to learn about feelings when our friends told us, "Don't let him know you like him." And, of course, there are those friends who've been in therapy for years and are a real pain in the butt because they are always "feeling this" and "feeling that." Or when we have problems in our relationship and our therapist tells us that the solution is for us to "share your feelings." Conversely, there are the porn stars who taught us a lot about feelings—be strong and silent. It's no wonder that we:

- rarely express our feelings to our lover
- don't like dealing with our own feelings or those of our lover
- feel guilty about some of our feelings, especially those involving our sexuality
- try to hide or deny our feelings (many of us even think this is healthy and a sign of being well adjusted. This explains why we tend to have high blood pressure, ulcers, difficulty sleeping, drink too much alcohol, and die earlier than women.)
- blame our lover for what we are feeling, such as, "You make me feel so miserable" and "You make me so angry."
- confuse our feelings with our thoughts (Thoughts are not feelings! For example, "I feel you don't like me" is not a feeling. This is a thought and should be expressed: "I do not think you like me." A general rule—when the phrase "I feel"

is followed by the word "that" you are expressing a thought and not a feeling.)
• pretend to be the strong, silent sexual fantasy

In spite of all this negative stuff about feelings, and even though we may not like to admit it, each and every one of us does have feelings. Naturally, there are times when you may not be able to name what you are feeling—but you are still feeling.

If you find it difficult to know what you are feeling, pay attention to your body. Most feelings are experienced in our bodies; for example, when you get frightened there may be a knot in your stomach or tightness in your throat. Feelings are also connected to your behavior. If you aren't sure how you feel, but you realize you are behaving in a certain way, you may be able to infer what you are feeling from this behavior. Making the connection between your behavior and your feelings is very useful. For example, we:

• shout when we are *angry*
• become silent and stop talking to our lover when we are *hurt*
• flirt when we are *attracted* to a guy
• get an erection when we are sexually *aroused*
• blush when we are *embarrassed*
• smile when we are *happy*
• pout when we are *unhappy*
• stop going to the gym with our lover because we are *jealous* when other men look at him

Once you recognize your feelings, you may then more clearly articulate your feelings with your lover:

I admired you when _____.
I'm so afraid to _____.
I get angry when _____.
I was annoyed when _____.
I'm really aroused when _____.
I feel betrayed when _____.

I'm curious as to why _____.
It disgusts me when _____.
I'm eager to go _____.
I was so enthused _____.
I feel embarrassed when _____.
I really enjoy _____.
I'm really excited that you _____.
It makes me so happy to _____.
I hope we _____.
It hurt me when _____.
I feel insecure when _____.
I was so inspired to _____.
I'm interested in _____.
I got jealous when _____.
I'd like it if you'd _____.
I love you so much!
I feel neglected when _____.
I feel such pride in _____.
I regret we didn't _____.
I was shocked when _____.
I'm deeply sorry about _____.
I'm suspicious when _____.

Activity

Hold hands with your lover and share a feeling about something that's really important to you. For example:

• "I got hurt last night when I touched you and you pulled away."
• "I was frightened last night when you got angry."

Men in Successful Relationships Use "I" Rather Than "You"

Using "I" is about sharing something important to you and in your life.

1. "I" should always be used when expressing your feelings to your lover (or to anyone else).
    • "I want a monogamous relationship with you."
    • "I would prefer a sexually open relationship."
    • "I don't want a dog."

2. "I" indicates that you are responsible for your own actions and for your own opinions.
    • "I feel neglected when I'm ignored at parties."
    • "I did not like that movie."
    • "I do not like you."
    • "I feel very unappreciated when I'm not taken seriously."
    • "I feel insulted when I'm patted on the head and treated like a child."

3. "I" affirms that you are united as a couple.
    • "How can I handle this issue better?"
    • "I want to respond to your fear of being abandoned."

Using "I," however, does make you vulnerable because you are sharing something about yourself—your feelings. This means you are taking a risk and could be hurt. That can be scary because getting hurt (being vulnerable) does happen, even in successful relationships. **Being Mr. Right means allowing yourself to become vulnerable in your relationship and with your lover.**

    • "I'm lonely when you spend so much time away."
    • "I was scared when you didn't call me after you promised that you would."
    • "I'm very anxious when we have an argument."

Using "I" with your lover is a good indication that trust is present in your relationship. Trust that he will not be frightened with what you share. Trust that he will not abuse what you have shared. Trust that he will not judge you for what you have shared.

Trust is confidence in your relationship, lover, and yourself. **Trust is the most important component of a successful relationship.**

- "I don't want you to leave."
- "I love you."
- "I'm frightened that you will reject me for all the things I have told you about my past."

Using "I" makes your relationship change and grow, but does not tell your lover what to do or demand that he change. "I" gives your lover a choice—he can decide whether to make changes.

Situation: Your lover comes home from work and talks about all the cute boys he has seen during the day.
- " I'm glad we talk during dinner, but I'm threatened by the way you talk about the cute guys at your office. "

Situation: Your lover cruises every guy on the street when the two of you are together.
- "I get concerned about our relationship when you stare at every well-built guy you see. I'd feel a lot better if you wouldn't do this when we are together."

Situation: You have plans to meet your lover and he always shows up late.
- "I get frustrated and then start to worry something has happened to you when you are late."

Activity

Both you and your lover practice using "I" statements. This will also help each of you hear what the other is really saying. Have a discussion about this activity when you have completed it.

Using "I" seems so easy, but it's not. It feels awkward and it takes practice to get comfortable saying "I."

"You" statements	"I" statements
You make me so mad.	I feel angry when you _____.

You are such a flirt.	I feel betrayed when you _____.
"You don't love me.	I feel neglected when you avoid me.
You piss me off!	I feel annoyed when you _____.
Must you always cruise?	I really feel insecure when you flirt.
You know everything!	I like when you're not an expert on everything.
You are so obnoxious.	I feel embarrassed when you _____.
"You must do _____.	I'd like it if you'd _____.

Activity
Men use "you" statements most of the time. Keep a written record of all the ways you use the word "you."

Most men prefer using "you" rather than "I" because it feels less risky and doesn't share as much about them. In other words, "you" doesn't make us vulnerable because "you" is about our lover.

1. "You" sounds as if you are asking him to change.
   • "You are always late."
   • "You never kiss me good night anymore."

2. Using "you" tells him what to do. No one wants to stay in a relationship if he is constantly being told what to do or being asked to change.
   • "You need to make the bed in the morning."
   • "You should get up earlier in the morning so you aren't always late for work."

3. Using "you" blames him.
   • "You always start the arguments."
   • "You are so defensive."

4. "You" is an attack and can make him defensive. Setting up defenses is what we do when we go to war. The battle lines will then be drawn, and the two men fight to win.

• "You are a selfish, mean person."
• "You are a lazy slob."
• "You are arrogant."

"You" is an attack, even if it is used in a question.

Situation: You and your lover arrive home after partying all evening and you say to him: "Do you have to be so wild at parties?" Your lover will hear this question as an attack:
• "You were drinking too much and hugging all the men."
• "You were on the make even though you came with me to the party."
• "You neglected me while you were flirting with the other men."
• "When we go to parties, you should spend more time with me, not drink so much, and stop coming on to everyone."

Men will also substitute the words "we," "all," "us," "they," and "everybody" for the word "you."

• "We don't want a dog."
• "Everybody says you are acting like an asshole."
• "They agree with me."
• "All my friends say a sexually open relationship doesn't work."
• "Everyone thinks you are obnoxious."
• "All gay men have a sexually open relationship."

MEN IN SUCCESSFUL RELATIONSHIPS LISTEN AND RESPOND WITH EMPATHY

Listening to your lover sounds easy; after all you have been listening to people your entire life. But listening is not quite as easy as it sounds. Our ability to listen lasts only about 15 to 20 minutes. After that our mind starts to wander. (Remember your teachers who talked on and on? How much did you remember at the end of the class?) We begin to think of other things we would rather be doing.

Think about yourself and how you listen to your lover. At the end of a conversation, how much do you remember about what he has said to you? Can you repeat what he just said to you? Probably not—because you are not really listening to him. So how can you become a better listener?

1. You need to listen carefully to what your lover is saying, what he is feeling, and what he did because of what he was feeling.

2. Listening means you are not speaking, not defending, and not criticizing what he is saying.

3. Listening means you have to stop:
   • planning on what you are going to say after he finishes talking
   • daydreaming
   • comparing your own personal experiences to his (I've had a rougher day than he has; he has had an easier life than I have)
   • reading his mind (he's only saying this to make me feel bad)
   • judging his comments (how stupid)
   • interrupting his comments
   • changing the topic
   • placating him by agreeing with him
   • hearing only what you want to hear (and not hearing what you interpret as being negative about you)

4. Listening means you also have to observe his body language and facial expressions. Is he frowning or smiling? Are his arms folded? Does he look upset? Is he turning away from you or facing you? Does he look engaged with you?

5. Listening means you try to:
   • see things as he sees them
   • accept what he is saying
   • identify with what he is saying
   • experience events as he experiences them

• feel what he is feeling—his joy, excitement, sadness, fear, suffering, etc.
• Listening requires that you repeat what you heard him say, giving him the opportunity to clarify what he said.

If you really care about your lover, you will want to really hear what he has to say and learn what this event really means to him. Even if he is complaining about something you did and the complaint seems unjust, exaggerated, and unfair—you need to listen and learn what is going on with this man you love.

Listening also means responding with empathy to what you have heard your lover say—which is even more difficult than listening.

Situation: Your lover has just come home and tells you he has been outed at work by a coworker. How can you respond with empathy?

1. Responding with empathy means you cannot:
   • ask questions ("What did he say?" or "When did he first suspect?")
   • tell him what to do ("You should talk with your supervisor immediately.")
   • change the topic ("That happened to our friend Bob when he was working for the city.")
   • ignore what he has said ("It's time for dinner.")

2. An empathetic response includes feelings. This focus on feelings encourages your lover to continue letting you know what is going on with him. An empathetic response shows you care and you really understand him.

Lover: "At work today, one of the men talked about me being gay in front of some of my coworkers."
You: "You sound very upset."
Lover: "Yes, I am."

3. An empathetic response invites your lover to "spill his guts." But he must feel safe enough to explore his situation and his feelings. The more you "hear" the unspoken feelings and communicate your understanding of him, the safer he will feel and the more he will share with you.

> **You:** "You must have been really scared."
> **Lover:** "Yes, I'm really scared. I'm afraid one of my coworkers might tell my supervisor. I'm not sure what to do."
> **You:** "It doesn't sound as if you are upset being "outed" to your coworkers, but concerned that someone will tell your supervisor."
> **Lover:** "Yes, that's true. I would like your help in figuring out what to do."

Activity

Have a friend tell you about a problem (which can be made up).

- Listen to what your friend is saying.
- Respond with empathy.
- Have your friend give you feedback to your responses by identifying how your comments made him or her feel.

After doing this activity several times, practice being empathetic with other friends. Then try to be empathic with people you dislike or with whom you are having a conflict. Empathy will also help you to learn about these people—usually there is an explanation for mean people being mean.

Activity

Now it's time to be empathetic with your lover. Schedule an hour twice a week with him. One hour belongs to him and the other hour belongs to you.

- During the first half-hour, one of you talks about what is going

on in his life—his needs, hopes, characteristics, disappointments (no blaming!), hurts, joys, plans, etc. He does not talk about the other one or about the relationship.
- The listener does nothing but listen in order to learn what is going on with this man he loves. He does not speak, does not defend, and does not criticize what his lover is saying.
- During the second half-hour, the listener gives immediate feedback to the talker about how the listener reacted to what was being said.

MEN IN SUCCESSFUL RELATIONSHIPS KNOW THERE ARE DIFFERENT INTERPRETATIONS OF THE SAME EVENT

When we finally meet a man and fall in love, everything is wonderful. Why does something that starts out feeling so good go downhill? Why do so many of our relationships become filled with faultfinding, arguments, frustration, hurt feelings, and anger? Why do we have arguments with this man we love? It would be much better if there were no disagreements and no arguments. But get real—this just isn't going to happen.

Many disagreements, arguments, and problems occur because of the interpretations we make of the events in our lives. It is important to recognize that interpretations of events are really just that and interpretations are your own creations. Many men in a relationship, however, either wrongly interpret a situation or have different interpretations of the same event. Following are some examples of the different ways interpretations can lead to problems in our relationships:

- **Dichotomous thinking**—interpreting events in extremes with no gray areas in between ("all or nothing")
  "Let me cook dinner, you always manage to screw it up."
- **Personalizing events**—interpreting your lover's behavior or feelings as a response to something you did
  "You seem so upset, what have I done wrong?"
- **Overgeneralization**—interpreting an event as having a greater impact on your life than it truly does
  "Since we don't have any money in our checking account, we

won't be able to do anything this weekend."
• **Filtering**—interpreting events so that everything is negative in your life
   "They never invite us for dinner, they must not like us."
• **Faulty thinking**—interpreting your experiences as being correct
   "Since I can't meet a man, I must be unattractive."
   "None of my relationships have ever worked out, I know it's because I don't know how to maintain a successful relationship."

When you stop to think about it, each situation you experience may have a variety of interpretations. Men in successful relationships know there are always different interpretations of the same event.

Activity
• Think of an event that caused an argument between you and your lover (or a friend).
• Identify your interpretation of the event that caused you to be angry.
• Then identify some of the other possible interpretations for that same event.
• Do you know which interpretation is correct?

Your interpretation of an event also determines what you are feeling. Interpretations are made so rapidly and so automatically that you may not even be aware you are interpreting; however, your feelings are a valuable signal to you that you are interpreting some event.

Situation: Your lover looks at a very attractive guy at a party.

   • Your interpretation: Wow, he finds that adorable guy cute, but he is my lover so he must find me just as attractive.
   • Your feeling: happy
   • Your interpretation: He finds that guy more attractive than me and is probably planning on meeting him when I'm not around.
   • Your feeling: hurt and angry

Situation: You have been dating Ed for a few months and one night he casually says he thinks the age difference between the two of you may cause problems in the future.

• Your interpretation: Ed sees me as "being too old."
• Your feeling: hurt and angry
• Your interpretation: Ed's previous lover was older and it didn't work.
• Your feeling: confused
• Your interpretation: Ed believes I may be thinking he is too young for me.
• Your feeling: concern
• Your interpretation: Ed is upset because I didn't want to go out dancing last night.
• Your feeling: worry

Situation: Your lover seems cold and irritated.

• Your interpretation: He is mad at me because I did something with a friend last night.
• Your feeling: annoyed
• Your interpretation: I haven't told him how much I love him for a couple of days.
• Your feeling: concern

Situation: Your lover comes home late from work.

• Your interpretation: He is rude and inconsiderate.
• Your feeling: anger
• Your interpretation: He is forgetful.
• Your feeling: disappointment
• Your interpretation: He may have been hurt in an accident.
• Your feeling: worry
• Your interpretation: He met a cute guy and went home with him.
• Your feeling: hurt

Activity

The different feelings you have for different interpretations will become clearer after doing this activity.

• Identify your interpretation of events that happen during one day. Make a list of the various feelings that occur with each interpretation.
• Then identify other possible interpretations of the same events. Make a list of the feelings that occur with these new interpretations.

Ryan and Ethan have been a couple for 10 years and there is a 15-year age difference between the two of them. They met in a gay bar one evening, started dating, and eventually became a couple. Ethan is a salesman at a large department store, works out in the gym, and likes being cruised by other men. Ryan is a reporter, enjoys his work, and loves his home. Ethan works longer hours than Ryan does and because of this he never gets time by himself. One day Ethan came home from work and asked for some time alone in the house.

Ryan started thinking, *Why doesn't Ethan want me to be home? Why does he want to be alone in the house?* And of course Ryan could have several interpretations to Ethan's request:

• Ethan doesn't love me anymore.
• Ethan is planning on bringing someone home for sex.
• Ethan really does just want some time alone.
• Ethan may want time alone to work on his projects without me around.
• Ethan wants to surprise me by cooking dinner.

Ryan, however, really believes that Ethan is planning on having sex in their home with someone he met at the gym. Ryan then gets angry and an argument begins. The argument escalates and both Ryan and Ethan say some nasty things to each other. At this point they put up their walls to protect themselves from being rejected—and from being vulnerable. Ryan then stops arguing and says nothing—giving Ethan the silent treatment.

Ethan begins to think, *There are other men out there, I don't need him. I could find someone closer to my age who wouldn't be so threatened every time I go out.* And Ryan starts thinking, *I'm so tired of the constant arguments, that's all we do is fight. At my age I don't need this aggravation.* Both begin to think of breaking up.

Neither Ryan nor Ethan is willing to take the risk of using "I" statements to share a feeling and become vulnerable. But the truth is that both of them are frightened. They had only been together two years at the time of this argument. It is really upsetting for both of them to think of breaking up. Ethan is confused (all he wanted was some time alone in the house). It is so painful for Ryan to think of all his relationship dreams crumbling. He wonders what he could say to make things better and to get Ethan to talk about it some more.

What could Ryan and Ethan have done differently to change this situation?

• Either one of them could use an "I" phrase and express a feeling.
"I *love* you and I'm *afraid* I might be losing you. I don't *want* this to happen. I would *like* to save our relationships. What can I do?"
• Ryan could respond with empathy to Ethan's request.
"You are asking for some time alone in the house and I understand. It must be frustrating to come home and want to be alone and I'm always present."
• Ryan could identify how he has interpreted Ethan's request and how that interpretation made him feel.
"I'm really upset by you wanting time alone. I have noticed you

are always talking on the phone with that cute guy you work with and whom I have never met. When you requested time alone, I began to think you were trying to get rid of me so you could be alone with him."

Now Ryan and Ethan can do the work of resolving this situation and saving their relationship.

MEN IN A SUCCESSFUL RELATIONSHIP TREAT THEIR LOVER AS THEIR BEST FRIEND

You interpret an event, this interpretation causes you to have a feeling, and that feeling causes a reaction—a behavior. And many of these behaviors are harmful to your relationship.

• You feel hurt, angry, betrayed, unappreciated—you start an argument with your lover.
• You feel hurt, jealous, insecure, or angry—you call your lover an "asshole."
• You feel angry your lover is cruising someone in a bar—you leave without him.
• You feel insecure, jealous, hurt, and angry—you treat your lover as if you don't like him.

Harmful behaviors are caused by what you are feeling. But it's not your feelings that are causing problems for you. Feelings are neither bad nor good. It's the harmful behaviors prompted by your feeling hurt, disappointed, angry, and sad that cause problems in your relationship. **These harmful behaviors, however, can be stopped.** For example, if you go dancing with your lover and become sexually aroused, you don't have sex with him on the dance floor. If you get a promotion at work, you don't jump up and down screaming out at the top of your lungs. When you learn to stop harmful behaviors, you are on your way to becoming Mr. Right.

The most important step in stopping those harmful behaviors is to know what you are thinking because your feelings come from your thoughts (which as you know can be an interpretation). Putting this into different words—your thoughts (interpretations) determine your feelings and your feelings determine your behavior. For example:

- If you think your lover is mad at you, you feel hurt and your behavior is to withdraw.
- If you think how lucky you are to have met such a wonderful man, you feel love and your behavior is to bring him flowers and cook him a special dinner.
- If you think nothing will work out between you and your lover, you feel sad and then you don't try to make your relationship work.
- If you think your lover is having an affair, you feel angry and then you may have an affair to get even, or you may get out of the relationship.
- If you think how sexy your lover looks, you feel aroused and you try to seduce him.
- If you think gay men don't want a monogamous relationship, you feel helpless and don't ask your lover to be monogamous.
- If you think "you can't teach an old dog new tricks," you feel hopeless and don't try anything new that might help your relationship become successful and you don't finish reading this book.

When you were dating your lover, your thoughts about him were positive, so you felt good about the relationship and probably smiled a lot. Do you still have the same thoughts? If so, you are still planning on spending your life with him. If not, that is part of why you no longer feel the same about him or the relationship. Certain thoughts can make you feel miserable, for example when your lover criticizes you, you start talking to yourself (usually silently) and then you start to feel hurt, disappointed, and angry. And other thoughts can make you feel great—the man you are dating tells you how much he loves you and your thoughts are about becoming a couple.

Activity

Think about your lover. Does he know what you think about him? Not just the things you tell him but the private stuff in your head. Would you want him to know? If you would, it's time to tell him. If not, it's time to change those thoughts!

I don't like to admit it, but I have behaved hurtfully to Christopher. For example, I raise my voice when I get upset. My method for stopping these behaviors is to change my thoughts, which then change my feelings, and therefore my behaviors change. My method for changing my thoughts is to think about "crazy people." "Crazy people" can do two things that noncrazy people cannot do: (1) they can read minds and (2) they can predict the future. I use "craziness" to help me change my harmful behaviors.

Christopher frequently leaves in the morning to collect rare tropical plants and usually comes home early in the afternoon. If he isn't home when it starts to get dark, I "know" he has had a car accident (my thought) and any second the state police will come to the door and give me the news (predicting the future). I start to get nervous (feeling) and stop doing the fun things I like to do during the day (behavior). When that starts to happen to me, I know I'm predicting the future (he has been killed) and I'm behaving like a "crazy person."

When I meet a nongay man I "know" he is homophobic (thought) and then feel cautious and start to withdraw (behavior). I'm reading this man's mind. That means I'm acting like a "crazy person." He may be homophobic or he may not. I really don't know since I can't read his mind.

When I start predicting the future or reading minds, I stop and remind myself I'm not crazy and I can't do these things. That helps, especially when I laugh at my craziness.

Thoughts that predict the future can be changed. If you are thinking, "my relationship isn't going to be successful because most relationships aren't," you are predicting your future. This prediction (thought) will certainly make you feel upset and this may cause you to do a harmful behavior, such as getting out of a relationship before you do any work to make it successful. Rather than predicting an unsuccessful relationship for your future, let's predict a different future—you and your lover will celebrate your silver wedding anniversary with your families and friends. With this as a prediction for your future, you will definitely be feeling happy. Which prediction is true? Which one is wrong? Do you know? Of course you don't know because you can't predict the future (you are not crazy). Nobody can do this, but so many people do predict their own future, experience feelings based on their predictions, and then behave as if their prediction is correct.

How often do you predict the future? In reality, many men act as if they can and they usually predict something negative rather than positive. Your prediction will have you feeling and behaving in a certain way—depending on your prediction. For example:

- **Prediction:** My lover is late for dinner because he is having an affair.
- **Feeling:** anger, sadness, hurt, or frustration
- **Behavior:** You call friends and go out cruising.

However, you can change your prediction (thought) and cause your feelings to change. You may then behave differently. For example:

- **Prediction:** My lover is late for dinner because he is working longer hours to make more money for our future together.
- **Feeling:** happiness, joy, or exhilaration
- **Behavior:** You keep dinner warm until he gets home.

Thoughts that come from reading other people's minds can also be changed. When your lover said no to having a joint-checking account, did you "know" the reasons why he said no? Some of your thoughts (interpretations) could be:

• He hasn't told me the truth about how much money he earns.
• He is thinking of breaking up.
• He doesn't trust me.
• He believes I'm financially unstable.
• He believes I'm not good at handling money.

All these examples are an attempt to read your lover's mind in order to explain why he said no. But the truth is that you really don't know why he behaved this way: You can't read his mind. But after trying to read his mind you felt rejected, became cautious, took fewer risks, and thought about getting out of your relationship.

Once you accept that you can't read minds, you are on the way to changing your feelings and your behaviors. The next time your lover says he doesn't want to have sex tonight, and you believe he is no longer attracted to you—laugh at yourself because you are reading his mind and acting like a "crazy person."

Feelings and behaviors can be changed if you change your thoughts. But many men wrongly believe their thoughts are outside of their control. Since you are in charge of your own brain, you can create certain thoughts, get rid of other ones, stop predicting the future, and stop reading minds. Start thinking of your lover as a kind, understanding, and wonderful person, and you will have great feelings about him. You are then acting like Mr. Right and treating your lover as your best friend.

Activity
• Identify the feelings you don't like and the thoughts you are having when you experience these feelings.
• Write each of these feelings and thoughts on a separate 3-by-5 card.
• Take each of your 3-by-5 cards and look at all your thoughts and the feelings that come from these thoughts.
• How many of these thoughts are 100% accurate? Be careful here—you may have had these thoughts for so many years that you now believe they are totally correct.

• Now try again, but instead of trying to figure out how accurate your thought is, ask yourself this question: *Is my thought helping me or hurting me?* For example, if you think your relationship isn't going to become successful, this thought is really hurting you because it is causing you to behave in a way that is not in your best interest.

MEN IN SUCCESSFUL RELATIONSHIPS FIGHT FAIRLY WITH THEIR LOVER

All couples have disagreements; however, Mr. Wrong tries to resolve these disagreements by "fighting to win." Fighting to win means fighting to prove you are "right" and your lover is "wrong." **Most men who fight to win have unsuccessful relationships.**

It is important to resolve disagreements with both men feeling good about the discussion, feeling good about the solution, feeling good about his lover, feeling good about himself, and feeling good about the relationship—this is "fighting fairly." In fighting fairly, those men who have learned how to be Mr. Right:

• share their feelings.
• use "I" statements rather than "you" statements
• listen to each other and respond with empathy
• know that events can be interpreted differently
• treat their lover as their best friend

At the end of their Caribbean cruise, both Ricky and Shawn went home knowing each wanted to see the other again. They continued the relationship by talking on the phone almost every day. They spent long weekends together in Chicago and Shawn spent his next summer vacation in Boston. After Shawn returned to Chicago, they missed each other and wanted to spend the rest of their lives together.

One evening Ricky phoned to say that a friend of his could get Shawn a teaching job in Boston and he wanted him to move there. Shawn was angry that Ricky didn't even consider moving to Chicago. A "fight" started that could have ended their relationship.

Shawn: "Why does it have to be your way? My teaching job is important to me and my friends are also important. I'm not going to leave Chicago and move to Boston."

Ricky: "I don't intend to leave a lucrative private practice and move to Chicago. That would be stupid. This relationship isn't going anywhere."

But the "fight" didn't end Ricky and Shawn's relationship. The "fight" continued, but it continued fairly.

Shawn: "But I don't want to lose you, I love you."

Ricky: "I love you too, and I want us to be a couple. But I want us to be a couple living together, not hundreds of miles apart, and I really want us to live in Boston."

Shawn: "I would be lonely moving so far away, starting a new job, and not having any of my friends near me for support. I really would like it if you moved to Chicago."

Ricky: "I understand this would be something new for you and it would be lonely for you. If you moved here, I will try really hard to be supportive and helpful."

Shawn: "Thanks, I really appreciate that you understand. If at all possible, I would like you to come to Chicago next weekend so we can talk more about living together."

Ricky: "I'll do that and I will also explore various medical practices in Chicago and see what is available."

Shawn: "I'd like that. If you don't find anything suitable, I still want us to be a couple and to live together. I will explore with you what it would be like for me to move to Boston. If I do move to Boston and am not happy living there, I still want to live with you. I would then want to explore other options, and I would not want you to say to me that you will only live in Boston."

Ricky: "I agree. I really do love you very much."

Learning how to be Mr. Right doesn't mean you or your lover is Mr. Perfect. There is no such creature! Chapter Three looks at accepting Mr. Right and not trying to change him into Mr. Perfect.

Chapter Three
Accepting Mr. Right

As we begin our relationship with Mr. Right, we both believe this relationship is going to be successful because we will:

• have a concern and a positive acceptance of each other
• be there for each other during the good and the bad
• be open, tender, trusting, and honest with each other
• share our excitement, joy, problems, and activities with each other
• share with each other the feelings, beliefs, and behaviors we don't share with everyone
• create the time to be alone with each other

However, many of us also believe that in this relationship, we will:

• express our needs and always have them met, such as "I want you to be with me tonight, holding me, cuddling together, and then having sex."

• have the same expectations, whether it's where we spend our vacation, buying new furniture, owning a second home, being monogamous, owning pets, or even adopting a child
• never have any disagreements, arguments, or fights
• be able to ask our lover to make changes, and he will agree to our requests

This type of relationship just doesn't exist because he will never be Mr. Perfect—even though you and Mr. Right may be perfect for each other. Even if he is Mr. Right, he will not be able to meet all of your expectations. Mr. Right is different from you—he has different expectations, likes and dislikes; he will usually behave differently in different circumstances, and he's not going to change just because you want him to change.

Mr. Right Is Different From You

While dating, the two of you don't see anything "wrong" with each other because you both seem so similar. You are very happy you have finally met "Mr. Right"—until he doesn't seem so similar and his differences become more obvious. I can't begin to recount the number of times I have heard, "He is so weird—he likes horror movies, sushi, science fiction, and he even likes football." And no matter how hard these men try, they just can't see how anyone can eat sushi or enjoy watching football. However, **men in successful relationships accept each other's differences— their goodness, craziness, weirdness, weaknesses, strengths, faults, happy side, and sad side.** So even if you don't like that he eats sushi or enjoys football, this man is your Mr. Right and it is important that you accept his differences.

Jeff and Gary are both 75 years old and have been a couple for 50 years. They are both now retired and live in Los Angeles, but they met in San Francisco while they were in the Navy. When Jeff and Gary began their relationship, they had a major difference between them—Jeff was an officer and Gary was an enlisted man. After they were discharged from the service, they continued to have differences—in their careers, attractiveness, money, and interests. "I love cooking and cleaning," said Jeff. Gary enjoys gardening. They both like to travel, but Jeff enjoys cruises and Gary prefers getting to where they are going as quickly as possible. Jeff loves large parties and Gary prefers small dinner parties. Gary prefers cats and Jeff prefers dogs. But Jeff and Gary have been a successful couple for 50 years—both men accept each other's differences.

Christopher sometimes calls me "anal retentive" because I'm so organized. I don't think of myself as being that organized, but in comparison to him I am super organized. But Christopher's memory can't be beat. He can remember everything—even things I said years ago. Which difference is better—organization or memory? The only answer in our relationship is—neither one.

This acceptance of those differences in Mr. Right is built on the recognition that even if there are things about him you don't like, he is still a wonderful man—he is your Mr. Right and you love him. There is something very interesting, however, about some of the differences between the partners in a male couple. **The differences that caused two men to be attracted to each other in the beginning may be the same differences that annoy them later in the relationship.**

Christopher and I are very different. He is playful, spontaneous, and boyish. On the other hand, I'm very organized, efficient, and stable. It was his "boyishness" that first attracted me to him and it was my "maturity" that he found attractive. So what differences do we now sometimes find annoying in each other?

Christopher: "Ken, let's go out for a cappuccino."
Ken: "No, I don't want to go out now. I just sat down to read a book."

Christopher: "I just thought going out now would be fun."
Ken: "I wish you had suggested that earlier."

Men in successful relationships recognize those formerly attractive and now annoying differences in each other as unique and special—as it was in the beginning. In order to help you do this, I have developed the concept of "stardom"—each lover is the "star" in the area that makes him special. One man in the relationship may be the "star" at having a more outgoing personality and the other in having most of the good looks. One lover may be the center of attention at a party and the other in their home. One may be the star cook in their relationship and the other may be the star gardener.

Christopher is the star in being boyish and I'm the star in being mature. This makes our differences special.

Being a "star" does not imply a judgment of good or bad on those differences. In other words, it is not better or worse to be boyish or mature in our relationship, that's just the way it is. **Men in successful relationships acknowledge, appreciate, and accept each other's special differences—which are the areas in which each is a "star."**

It may be difficult accepting your lover's differences as being special and recognize those differences as making him a star. But I would like to ask every man reading this book **to look at his own differences and those of his lover and to accept them as being unique in his relationship—and then tell his lover those areas in which he is a star.** It is important that each man in the relationship is a star at something. Both men, however, have to agree on each other's stardom, feel good about their own stardom, and accept and enjoy each other's stardom.

Another difference between Christopher and me is in the area of creativity. I know his artistry is one of the traits I found very attractive when we met. That difference, however, had the potential of causing disagreements for us, had I not realized how much I appreciate and value it. I accept and acknowledge that Christopher is the star in the creative area.

A few months ago, our local newspaper wanted to interview us on our various "achievements" since moving to Florida—Christopher for his tropical garden, and me for being the author of several books, including *Mr. Right Is Out There*. Christopher is known in our community for his garden, I'm less well known as a "gay author." The article had the potential for me to outshine Christopher's "creative stardom." I'm not really creative in the same sense he is—I don't want to be viewed as an artist, I like being viewed as a professor. It took a few minutes of discussion using "I" statements and responding with empathy for us to agree that an article should only be written about one of us.

In working with men in successful relationships, I have observed that they rarely have conflicts, arguments, or fights because they:

1. accept their differences as being special
2. agree they are both stars and have their own stardom
3. talk about where and when those differences will "shine"
4. enjoy watching the other shine

Many differences are easy to accept—gardening versus cooking, travelling on ships versus planes, having large parties versus dinner parties, and even having cats versus dogs. In the real world of male couples, however, some of those qualities that make him the star can really be quite annoying and much more difficult to accept.

SOME DIFFERENCES ARE MUCH MORE DIFFICULT TO ACCEPT AS SPECIAL

SOME DIFFERENCES ARE WRONG FOR YOU

It is crucial to indicate that many unsuccessful relationships occur because Mr. Right had qualities that we didn't like when we met him—but we didn't care. If he drank too much, partied all the time, didn't want to work, or hated dogs, we believed our love for him would help him to change. But he didn't change and after a couple years, we began to realize that he was really Mr. Wrong. There are men whose differences are unacceptable to you and this makes him your Mr. Wrong. For example, a yes answer to the following questions could indicate that your lover might really be "Mr. Wrong:"

• Does he break or throw things when he gets angry?
• Does he easily lose his temper?
• Is he jealous of your friends or family?
• Does he demand to know where you have been when you are not with him?
• Does he accuse you of cruising if you talk with another man?
• Does he drink or take drugs almost every day or go on binges?
• Does he ridicule you, make fun of you, or put you down?
• Does he think it's acceptable to have a physical fight with you?
• Do you like yourself less when you are with him?
• Do you ever find yourself afraid of him?

It is important to acknowledge there are some differences that are wrong for you and that you will never be able to accept. If those differences make you feel badly and no matter how hard you try you just cannot accept them, you should not be in a relationship with this man—he is Mr. Wrong for you.

"Why the hell didn't you do last night's dishes before now? You've got to be the laziest SOB I've ever lived with. I'm going out with my friends, and when I get home the house had better be clean." This is typical of the way Lenny talked to Bob. Bob finally got out of this relationship.

Steve and Will tried for two years to make their relationship work. Steve's an alcoholic who kept promising Will that he would go to AA, but never did. He tried to stop drinking, but he wasn't able to. Will tried to accept that he was in a relationship with an alcoholic, but he couldn't. They fought constantly about this issue. Steve's alcoholism was not acceptable to

Will. Will finally admitted that to himself and to Steve and got out of the relationship.

SOME DIFFERENCES ARE ANNOYING

But accepting each other's differences and recognizing some differences as being special doesn't mean you have to like all of each other's differences. There are some differences he didn't do while you were dating; in fact, some differences don't show up until months after you start living together. For example, Mr. Right may now:

- not shower daily
- forget to flush the toilet
- burp during dinner
- bite his nails
- fart during sex

And years after you became a male couple, Mr. Right is different from the Mr. Right you dated—he has become older, his interests have changed, his body is heavier, he enjoys playing cards rather than dancing, and he is now retired. He is different from the man to whom you made a commitment, and you are not going to like all of these changes. He didn't snore when he was 25, but at 50 he may start to snore. At one time he did enjoy going out to the clubs; now he would rather sit in a chair and read a book. And with retirement, he is home all day, and if you also retire, the two of you are home together—all day! But he is still your Mr. Right— he is the man you love. However, you do find some of his differences really annoying. And there is nothing wrong with that. In spite of what you may have read or what a therapist may have told you—**unconditional love doesn't exist.**

It would be nice if you could request that he change these annoying behaviors and for him to agree, but relationships just aren't that easy. Your troubles begin when you try to change your lover. Remember—no man appreciates unsolicited comments on his faults, especially from his lover.

Does this mean you have to live with behaviors that are really annoying? No, you don't. But I don't believe you should give up on the relationship just because he has annoying differences. It is amazing how many men I have talked with who have left relationships because Mr. Right cracked his knuckles or snored. But I also don't believe you have to live with and put up with differences that really annoy you. There are some changes we all want our lover to make.

Activity

Make a list of your lover's annoying habits and traits from the most annoying to least (If you fear he will read it, destroy it after you have finished).

REQUESTING CHANGES IN SOME DIFFERENCES

Men in successful relationships do ask their lover make some changes.

Christopher is so much more creative than I am in making our home look beautiful. He always tells me when I do something nice, but I very rarely tell him how beautiful the house looks. When I don't say something about what he has done, I know he feels hurt. He has asked that I occasionally tell him how much I appreciate all the work he does to keep our home so beautiful. I have identified this difference as something I need to work on and to change.

Ricky and Shawn had regular arguments every Saturday morning about how to spend their weekends. Ricky's work as a physician keeps him in the office at least 50 hours a week, and he wants to do fun things on weekends. Shawn, however, wants to first do their entire household chores before making any plans to do anything else. It was usually late morning before they both agreed on what to do, greatly frustrating both of them. Ricky finally asked if they could talk every Thursday night about any differences that were upsetting to either of them, which included what to do on the weekends. Shawn agreed and this simple change turned Saturday from a day they dreaded into a day they eagerly anticipated.

But demanding that your lover change, criticizing him, fighting with him, giving him the silent treatment, yelling at him, rolling your eyes, or nagging him to stop biting his nails or farting during sex isn't going to work and could end your relationship. Nobody likes to have to admit he did something wrong or caused problems in the relationship. If his behaviors are criticized, your lover will feel attacked and get angry and the tendency will be for him to become defensive and attack back. "It just happened, it isn't my fault." "You are trying to get me to be something I'm not." He may become sarcastic, get quiet and withdraw, walk away, pretend to forget what was said and ignore it, or do something to get even. He will resist your efforts to change him and will redouble his efforts to prove that he can't be changed. **But your lover may choose to change if you:**

- identify the difference as a problem for you
- explain how this difference makes you feel
- honestly explain why this difference upsets you

But he will *not* change if you:

- pass judgment on the difference
- place a value on the difference
- view him as the bad guy
- call him "lazy"
- accuse him of being wrong

This does not mean you are being a martyr or a doormat because you identify this as a problem for you—because it is your problem. **Your difference is causing you to have a problem with your lover.** You are different from your lover since you don't bite your fingernails, don't snore, and you don't burp during dinner. If you both did those things there probably wouldn't be a problem. Who is to say which difference is correct?

• I know I act a little crazy when you snore during the night. It upsets me because it keeps me awake—I also know this is my problem.
• I know you are in a hurry in the morning, but my need for personal hygiene makes me feel anxious when you don't shower.
• I really get upset when you bite your nails. I don't know why this bothers me, but it does. You have also said it bothers you, what can I do to help you to stop biting your nails?
• When you burp during dinner I get really embarrassed. I know we both laugh about it, but my laughter hides my embarrassment.
• I know you can't help farting, but this creates a problem for me. It takes the excitement out of having sex with you.
• I do know you are concerned about the environment and trying to save water by not flushing the toilet, but I find myself going into the bathroom and flushing the toilet after you use it. This is making me feel used.

GUIDELINES FOR REQUESTING CHANGES

Lance and Al have been together for 12 years. Lance is a lawyer and likes his life to be fairly organized; Al is an interior designer and is comfortable with some chaos. During the first year together they realized they were both very busy in their professional lives, but they did plan to have dinner together every evening. That was their "together time" to talk about important events occurring in their lives.

This agreement worked for awhile, but then Al began to get home from work late. Lance began to realize Al was always late—not only for dinner, but for almost everything. Lance kept telling Al how this bothered him and Al would respond that Lance's punctuality was irritating to him. But this difference wasn't always a problem: When they first met Lance's punctuality was very appealing to Al and Lance found Al's "free spirit" appealing. Over time, however, these appealing differences became annoying differences.

When it was dinnertime and Al wasn't home yet, Lance got really angry. Al asked Lance not to wait for him and to go ahead and eat and just leave his dinner in the refrigerator. Lance, however, would sit and wait for Al. When Al finally got home, their time together was not very pleasant.

1. Identify the difference that is causing a problem: Lance needs to communicate with Al to let him know there is a difference between the two of them. Lance is always punctual and it upsets him when anyone is late. Al really doesn't think being late or early is a big deal. Lance took responsibility for his problem by using an "I" statement.

Lance: "I know my need for punctuality in myself as well as in others does cause problems for me. But I really don't know what to do when you are late for dinner."

2. Explain how this difference makes you feel: Lance shares with Al what he is feeling.

Lance: "I get really upset (feeling) and then I get angry (feeling) and that isn't good for me or for us. I would like some help in resolving my problem." Lance's previous solution was to burn Al's dinner. This behavior, however, is very manipulative and will certainly not "make" Al change. Manipulative behaviors can also destroy their relationship.

3. Listen and respond with empathy: Al does respond to what Lance has said, but his response is not an empathetic response.

• No matter how clearly Lance says this is his problem and no matter how much he uses an "I" statement, Al views this as an attack on his behavior and responds *defensively*.

Al: "I have to work late and there isn't anything I can do about it—so get off my back."

• Al may respond that he knows nonpunctual people (including him) upset Lance, but he gives a vague response.

Al: "I'll try harder." or "I don't know what to do."

4. Repeat problem: Since Al did not respond empathetically, Lance needs to repeat what he has said.

    Lance: "I do know you have to work late, but I get upset and angry when you are late. Having dinner together to talk about our day is important to me."

    • Al finally hears Lance and responds empathetically:

    Al: "I know my being late upsets you because having dinner together and talking is important to you. It is also important to me."

5. Acknowledge the empathetic response:

    Lance: "I do appreciate that you know I'm upset when you are late. I really would like us to come up with a solution that will help me when you are going to be late for dinner. Even though this is my problem, I'm concerned it will cause a problem for the two of us."

6. Propose solutions: It does help to avoid thinking there is only one possible solution. Spend some time thinking of all sorts of ways to handle the problem and don't ignore or criticize solutions you don't like. Any proposed solution must be acceptable to both Al and Lance. Al does respond with a solution:

    Al: "I really don't want you to be upset. It would be fine with me if you would call me before we close the office to see if I'm running late. If I'm going to be late, I would prefer that you go ahead and eat without me and put my dinner into the refrigerator for me to eat when I get home. Then I would like us to spend the rest of the evening together—not answering the phone, just the two of us."

7. State solutions in behavioral terms: It is best that any proposed changes be stated in behavioral terms—behavioral terms explain exactly what will occur, such as:

    Lance: "I will call you 30 minutes before your office closes and if you are going to be late coming home, I will go ahead and eat dinner. But I would then like to have at least an hour together every night so we can share our activities and be affectionate with each other."

8. **Reach agreement**: The next step is for both to agree to the change.

Al: "That sounds good to me."

Lance: "I will call you at 4:30 to see if you are running late. If you are, I will eat without you. Then when you get home, I will sit down with you while you are having dinner."

Al: "I would like that. After I finish dinner, I would like it if we could go to bed together to talk and to cuddle. If we both get horny, it would be great to have sex."

ASKING FOR AND OFFERING HELP

In the above example, Lance asked Al for help with his problem. Asking for help, receiving help, and offering to help requires both men to be able to appreciate and accept each other's differences.

Glen and Mike are both 35 years old and have been together for eight years. Shortly after moving in together, Glen saw Mike in the kitchen wearing an apron, making a cheese quiche for their breakfast. He began to explain to Mike that there was a "right and wrong way to make a quiche." He became critical of Mike's cooking abilities. Mike firmly told Glen he knew how to cook. A little later, Mike served a burned quiche for breakfast. That quiche could have been the end of their relationship—but instead they laughed. But the next time Mike made breakfast, he asked Glen to help and he agreed. Mike was glad to have Glen's help. Today, Mike makes the "world's best quiche" and they continue to laugh about their "first quiche together."

Of course, asking for help means acknowledging that your lover is better than you are in *those areas*. However, acknowledging that their lover might be better at some things is very difficult for many men.

Even in areas where I'm exceptionally competent, I frequently ask Christopher for his help. In writing certain parts of this book—in particular the chapter on power and control—I needed his help. Isn't it interesting that I—someone who likes to be in control—was having trouble with that chapter? I hated to ask Christopher for help because that meant giving up control. His suggestions and ideas, however, pushed me to do even better in writing that chapter (I hope you agree).

When you observe your lover is having trouble in a certain area, wait and see if he accepts your help after you offer it. He may want to struggle a little longer or get his ideas more organized before he is ready to accept your help. Furthermore, helping him without permission is controlling, which can harm a relationship.

Making the offer to help him is easy, but actually helping him isn't always so easy. Just because you are helping him in an area where he is not as good as you does not mean that:

• you should take charge and do it for him
• you can treat him in a condescending manner
• he is incompetent. If you believe your lover is incompetent, then you have not accepted his difference and this is something you will have to work on.

For example, his asking for your help in improving his cooking ability doesn't mean you are a "gourmet cook," and even if you are, that doesn't make him your assistant. Helping your lover means the two of you will work together to prepare a meal.

When Christopher read this manuscript he said, "You are writing the way you lecture at the university. It's too wordy." He did not put down my writing style, and he made sense. His input helped me to write differently.

Be supportive while helping your lover with his problem and when he has accepted your help and wants to change. Anticipate that he will be successful—that way he will feel successful. In couples therapy, I often help one of the men with some difference he has identified as a problem only to have his lover say, "Yeah, it's a great idea, but he'll never do it." When that happens I know (1) this couple has to learn how to support each other and (2) the other lover has to learn how to give up being controlling (which is discussed in Chapter Six).

Activity
• Describe in writing one difference in your lover that is causing a problem for you. Your lover should do the same.
• Share this difference with each other.
• Talk about what changes each of you will make so your difference will stop causing a problem for your lover.
• Ask for whatever help you need in order to make this change a reality.
• Each of you write how you will change so that the difference no longer causes a problem for the other. Don't rush this step; it may be difficult.

SOME DIFFERENCES THAT CAN CAUSE PROBLEMS FOR MALE COUPLES

BEING IN DIFFERENT STAGES IN THE COMING OUT PROCESS
When most of us were young and beginning to realize we were "homosexuals," we had such fears as:

• No one will like me (love me).
• My parents will reject me.
• I will have no friends.
• I will grow old alone and be lonely.
• I cannot have a successful career and be gay.
• I will lose my job.
• I will never have a successful relationship.

When Philip was in high school he came out to his mother.

One of her first concerns was that he would grow old alone—meaning he would not have a wife and children to take care of him in his old age. Philip went to the library to read about "homosexuality," and all the books confirmed his mother's fears. He'd spend the rest of his life cruising bowling alleys, looking for young men, eventually dying with no one at his bedside.

Many gay men are closeted because they have not yet worked through these fears (their own internalized homophobia). Some of these closeted men never form long-lasting relationships while others do meet Mr. Right and live with him, only to spend a lot of time and energy making sure their families believe they are just good friends. Members of their family never think of these closeted gay men as a couple; therefore, they never share in the joys in their lives.

Jeff and Gary have been a couple for 50 years and have lived together for about 45 years. They have a beautiful three-bedroom home; they sleep together in one bedroom and use the other two bedrooms for their out-of-town friends. However, when any family member visits, they pretend to sleep in separate bedrooms. They believe their families think they are "just good friends who have never found a wife." They have lived this lie for so long they really believe their families believe the lie. I don't, and neither did any of their friends Christopher and I met while visiting them. It is important to both Jeff and Gary to maintain the facade of heterosexuality.

Truth is the foundation for all relationships. Truth helps us to have a closer, more meaningful relationship, including our relationship with our family. Being truthful, however, means giving up pretending to be somebody you are not. Coming out to ourselves and to our friends, relatives, and parents is part of the process of getting close to others and of building a family. It means sharing our real self and our relationship with Mr. Right with others.

Coming out is essential to having a supportive family. Many of us do have our parents and siblings as part of our lives. Some of us also have children, adopted children, or foster children. Almost all of us have our gay and lesbian friends who have become our family. And others of us include our nongay friends as part of our family. **I believe having a supportive family helps to make male couples successful.**

You might be wondering why the topic of "coming out" is discussed in a chapter about differences. Frequently the two men in a relationship are in different stages of the coming out process and this difference can cause problems.

Arnold is a closeted lawyer and Larry is a travel agent who came out when he was 16. The couple rarely fights, unless it is about Arnold's closeted life, such as when Larry is not invited to a party for the partners at the law firm or when Arnold visits his family without Larry. They have many gay friends and socialize exclusively with them. Arnold does socialize after work with his friends at the law firm, but never includes Larry. Larry is active in the gay community where they live, but Arnold refuses to attend any of these gay events if there is a possibility nongay people will also be attending. Larry is frequently angry that Arnold doesn't come out of the closet. He threatens to "blast" Arnold out of the closet, but never does. This difference in their stage of the coming out process eventually ends the relationship between these two men.

If you are like Arnold and this is causing problems between you and your lover, now is the time to identify this as a problem and start working on changing this difference. Select a close nongay friend, a sibling, cousin, grandparent, or a parent and start the process.

1. You may be anxious because you predict how this person will react to your "homosexuality." Stop acting crazy and actually find out.

   • "I have been avoiding telling you something very important about me and I have now decided I would like you to know I'm gay."

2. Because you value this person, you will be concerned about the effect your coming out will have on your relationship. Now listen to this person's response. There will always be a response to coming out. For example:
• "I'm very angry that you waited so long to tell me. Didn't you trust me?"

3. Don't apologize. Being gay is nothing to apologize about. If you decide to be truthful and come out to your mother and she says, "What did I do wrong?" you can say:
• "Mom, what you did was right because I turned out to be a great son who loves you and wants to share with you who I am."

Being truthful with this person doesn't mean you have to share everything about your life. Your sexual behaviors can remain personal. Remember that being gay is more than being attracted to a man and having sex with a man; being gay is about being in love with a man and being a male couple. It is easier to be honest with others when you are talking about love rather than about sex! This doesn't make people as uncomfortable as a discussion about having sex with men. (Many ultrareligious people do not know how to respond to the question, "Does your religion say its wrong for me to love a man?")

Now give this person enough time to talk with you about what this means to your relationship with him or her.

BEING IN A LONG-DISTANCE RELATIONSHIP
Shawn had been looking for a lover for several years—and nothing ever lasted.

"I meet a guy, we date a few times, and then it ends. But then I went on this gay cruise and I met Ricky from Boston right there in the middle of the ocean. We talked and talked and both of us knew there was something special about our relationship. We decided to have sex the first night we met, which I usually don't do that soon. But I'm convinced the only effect that may have had was a positive one; we had only five nights left before the cruise ended and I think sexual compatibility needed to be determined quickly before anything long-distance was considered.

"We talked on the phone almost every day after we went home and he also came to Chicago for long weekends. We made plans for me to spend my summer vacation in Boston.

"I returned to Chicago just before Labor Day. We missed each other and wanted to spend our lives together. He called a week after I returned to tell me a friend of his could get me a teaching job in Boston and he wanted me to move there as soon as possible.

"I was angry that he didn't even consider moving to Chicago. I almost ended the relationship over his being insensitive to my needs. But after 15 years together, I'm glad I didn't."

Gay men always seem to find Mr. Right while on vacation! Or we'll meet someone in our own town only to find out he lives hundreds of miles away. Then we start running up enormous phone bills and travel expenses as we visit each other because we believe we have finally found Mr. Right.

As if relationships weren't complicated enough, these men are now in a relationship in which they:

• don't spend a lot of time together
• really don't get to know each other
• may not be able to afford the expenses involved in maintaining a long-distance relationship
• get frustrated with not seeing each other

Obviously these long-distance relationships require extra

work. The couple has to work at communicating as often as possible by phone, mail, or e-mail. They have to work on trusting each other when doing activities that might threaten the relationship. When they are together, they have to remember to do "normal" things as well as special things, resolving the problems that arise between them, and acknowledging and accepting that they:

- live in different places
- have different friends
- may even have different lifestyles

In spite of differences and the extra work involved, however, many male couples have been able to build a solid, happy, successful relationship from a connection that began on a cruise and developed over months of frequent flyer miles.

BEING WITH MR. RIGHT WHO LOVES GOSSIPING

It's natural to talk about our lover to our friends and family, and they in turn will talk about him to us, but this talking often leads to gossiping about our relationship. Worse than that, we trash, "dish," and put down our lover. Many of us also allow our family and friends to speak out against our lover. Gossiping has caused many relationships to become unsuccessful .

Remember that your lover will eventually find out whatever you or your friends and family say about him—he always does. He will resent you when he learns you have made, or allowed others to make, negative comments about him or that you have been sharing what he has said in confidence and discussing problems in the relationship. Not only will he resent you, he will also learn he can't trust you. **Trusting each other is essential in a successful relationship.**

This doesn't mean you shouldn't talk and share with friends and family. For example, if your lover learns you have been telling people how great he is, building him up, and even bragging about him, he will feel closer to you, trust will be reinforced, and he will feel great about being in a relationship with you. Knowing you are loyal and that you believe in him is essential in a successful relationship. But you shouldn't share relationship or lover problems with others (of course, this doesn't mean your therapist). When you talk about your lover, the conversation is one-sided—your side is doing all the talking—and he looks like the bad guy. His version would probably be just the opposite of yours. If you have a habit of complaining to your friends about your lover, it is time to stop. A good rule of thumb is to never say anything to anyone you wouldn't say directly to your lover.

This doesn't mean your family and friends aren't entitled to their opinions, but it doesn't give them the right to say negative things about your lover. If anyone does speak negatively, you should tell the person it is not acceptable for him or her to say those things. This includes criticisms and jokes. Too often we allow and even participate in joking about our lover. On the other hand, if you speak positively about your lover, negative comments from others will be minimal. Other people will know how you feel about him and will be more hesitant to say negative things about him. Furthermore, the way others view your lover will most likely improve based on your positive input.

Even though we are different from each other and may even have different wants, needs, wishes, and hopes, we do expect Mr. Right to fulfill our expectations for being a couple. In Chapter Four, we explore fulfilling these expectations.

Chapter Four
Fulfilling Mr. Right's Expectations

Although there are many reasons to become a couple, a primary reason for most gay men is that we cannot meet some of our most basic expectations on our own—they must be met by another man. These include our expectations for affection, emotional intimacy, sexual excitement, recreational companionship, nurturing, and admiration. When we meet someone whom we believe can fulfill these important expectations, he becomes our Mr. Right, we fall in love, and we hope to spend the rest of our lives with him.

Men in successful relationships (1) know each other's expectations (wants, needs, wishes, or hopes) and (2) have agreed to fulfill each other's expectations (wants, needs, wishes, or hopes). Many men do not seem to know this, which helps to explain why many of our relationships become unsuccessful.

Activity
I prefer to use the word "expectations" rather than "needs" because most men do not like to admit we have needs—it sounds

needy. We find it easier to identify what we expect from our lover—it sounds more powerful. For example, look at the following questions:

• What is an important need for you in this relationship? "I need him to be there for me in times of stress."
• What is an important expectation for you in this relationship? "I expect him to be there for me in times of stress."

The answers are really the same, but the first one implies a dependency more than the second answer. Most of us do not like to admit we are dependent on our lover to meet our needs—even though we are. (Even when we get angry with him when he isn't there for us, we don't like to admit we need him). The second answer sounds as if we know what we want in our relationship—we expect him to be there for us in times of stress. You have to decide which word is best for you—expectation, need, want, wish, hope, etc. The important thing is that you both know what you want and expect from the other because if those important expectations, wants, needs, wishes, or hopes aren't met, the relationship will not become successful.

Having a successful relationship, therefore, should be quite easy. We must begin our relationship (1) knowing each other's expectations and (2) wanting to fulfill each other's expectations. The truth, however, is that we frequently begin a relationship not knowing or inaccurately perceiving our lover's expectation and **these unknown or inaccurately perceived expectations create the problems in our relationships**. These problems occur because your lover may not want to fulfill your expectations once he really knows them, and you may not want to fulfill his once you really know them. Not fulfilling each other's expectations does lead to an unsuccessful relationship.

EXPECTATIONS

You see him across the room and walk over to introduce yourself. You are surprised to find you have lots to talk about—books, travel, what you do for a living, where you went to school, hobbies, favorite movies, etc. You both like what you hear and you see each other as being special; therefore, the two of you make plans to see each other again. Your first date with him is great, and so are your next few dates. As you continue to date, you both learn enough about the other to make a decision whether to continue seeing each other. For example: Christopher and I learned on our very first date that

• Christopher was an artist, in school on a scholarship, studied late most evenings, liked to dance, enjoyed "weird" (John Waters) movies, was very intelligent, and boyish.
• Kenneth was a professor at a university, liked to get up early in the morning to write, was professionally established, liked to travel, enjoyed old (black and white) movies, and was very organized.

Based on this information, Christopher and I decided to go out on a second date.

While dating you both begin making judgements as to whether or not the other is really your Mr. Right. These judgments are based on what you want (expect) in a lover and in a relationship. Your first glance, first touch, first kiss, and the first time you have sex all play into your expectations. There are expectations for living together, your sex life, vacations, a commitment to monogamy, pets, and shared interests. You expect him to be there when you need someone to talk with, laugh with, and cry with; a lover who cheers for your success and who is there for you when you fail. Your judgements of this man will help you know if you want to continue dating him.

After our first few dates, Christopher and I each knew the other could not meet some of his expectations, such as:

• Christopher could not meet my expectations for having a lover who would (at that time) be able to travel, take overnight trips, and share expenses.

• I could not meet Christopher's expectations for having a lover who would stay up late and then sleep late in the mornings and socialize comfortably with his school friends.

Our judgements of each other's expectations, however, helped us decide we wanted to continue dating.

Of course you will not know from the first date, or even the second date, if either one of you can meet the important expectations of the other. However, making judgements about each other's expectations is really necessary in order to prevent continuing to date a man who is really Mr. Wrong. But knowing each other's important expectations is essential prior to deciding to become a male couple.

The two of you will have many problems later in the relationship if your important expectations are not discussed early in the relationship. The success of our relationship is based on knowing and agreeing to fulfill each other's expectations, while not having our mutual expectations met causes disagreements and conflicts. **Men in successful relationships have always been honest from the very beginning about their important expectations for being a couple.**

Many men who have been honest in their relationships still have problems because they didn't discuss topics they considered sensitive while they were dating.

• We talk about our favorite movies and books, our jobs, places we have been, our families, etc., but we rarely talk about our dreams, desires, wants, hopes, and expectations. Dating is a time to get to know each other, to ask questions, to hear different opinions. As we continue to date and get more serious, we should ask:
  • Where would we eventually like to live?
  • If we own a house, will it be in both names? If we lease an apartment, will both our names be on the lease?
  • Will we be "out" to both of our parents? Will we pretend to share different bedrooms when our parents visit?
  • Will we be out to others? Nongay friends? Employers?

• Will we combine our incomes?

• Will we have a joint checking account?

• Will we equally share our living expenses, even if one of us makes more money?

• Will we make a commitment to monogamy?

• Will children from a previous relationship live with us? Spend time with us? When?

• Should we have children? Our own? Adopt? Foster children?

• Should we have pets? A cat? A dog? Something else?

• Who does what household chores?

• How will decisions be made?

• We made certain assumptions about each other's expectations, therefore we rarely talked about such assumptions as:

  • We will spend the holidays together.

  • We will both do the laundry.

  • We will sleep in the same bed.

• We tried to make a good impression, so we indirectly gave each other information that may have been inaccurate about our expectations. For example:

  • You pick up the check for dinner: He has learned you have money, and if you become a couple, you will pay for the fun things you do together.

  • You telephone him before he calls you: He has learned you will take care of him so he doesn't have to be responsible for himself.

  • You invite him to spend the night at your apartment rather than offering to stay at his place: He has learned you will want him to move in to your apartment.

  • He tells you he loves your cat: You have learned he will help take care of the cat.

  • He makes the bed in the morning: You have learned he will help with the household chores.

  • He offers to pick you up in his car after work: You have learned he will take care of you.

If either of you didn't like what you were learning about the other, you probably would stop dating. However, since you both liked what you learned, you begin thinking, "This guy is great. The cat's not going to be a problem when we move in together, and I like that we will share the household chores." And he's thinking, "I finally found someone who will take charge and will take care of me."

So the two of you continue dating, become a couple, move in together, and the disagreements and arguments begin because:

- He doesn't want the cat sleeping in the same bed with the two of you.
- He tells you he is too busy to pick you up after work, and you can take the bus home.
- He makes a list of the household chores that have to be done each week.
- You tell him how much he owes for his half of the household expenses.
- You won't call his parents and make excuses for him when he doesn't want to visit them on the weekend.

These disagreements, arguments, and eventually the ending of the relationship occurs because you and your lover had unknown or inaccurately perceived expectations when you became a couple. **Men in successful relationships know each other's relationship expectations and have agreed to fulfill them, which becomes their "relationship contract."**

OUR RELATIONSHIP CONTRACT

The main reason we don't become a successful male couple and "live happily ever after": **Each man begins the relationship with his own individual relationship contract of expectations and these two individual relationship contracts are unknown or inaccurately perceived by the other.** This happens because we believe he knows our expectations (which he doesn't) and he believes that we know his expectations (which we don't) and we both act as if we have agreed to fulfill each other's expectations (which we haven't).

Eventually our lover does something that violates what we assumed he promised, and disappointments occur, followed by arguments and fights. You probably know what happens next: Each of us starts working to change the other into the Mr. Right we thought we were getting.

Many of us spend the early years of our relationship trying to change our lover. We threaten, make promises, get angry and fight even more, and finally break up. Most of us have formed relationships that eventually break up because our individual relationship contracts of expectations were not fulfilled and we became disappointed with our lover and with the relationship.

Knowing all of this, it isn't surprising that our relationships frequently don't work. It has nothing to do with being gay or being men, it's simply the fact that we didn't fulfill each other's relationship contract. Perhaps if you were open about your expectations, he might not have agreed to this relationship. Perhaps if you knew his expectations, you may have gotten out of the relationship before either one of you called yourselves "boyfriend."

Glen and Mike are both 35 years old and met through mutual nongay friends, they have now been together for eight years. Glen designs computer programs for a large corporation and Mike works as a legal secretary in a law firm. On their first Christmas as a couple there was a disagreement that led to a big argument. Each of these men had always spent Christmas with their respective parents and siblings. Both came into the relationship with an expectation of bringing his new boyfriend "home" on this holiday. The argument continued for days, neither one having a resolution to their different expectations.

THE RELATIONSHIP CONTRACT MUST BE KNOWN AND AGREED ON

When two men decide to become a couple, they make a commitment to each other. This commitment is a promise to do the necessary work to make the relationship successful. No one, how-ever, should make a commitment to do this work until they have a "job description," which is described in our relationship con-tract. The relationship contract includes both your expectations—what he can expect from you and what you can expect from him. **Men in successful relationships know and have agreed to the con-tent of the relationship contract**; in other words, the men in suc-cessful relationships know and have agreed to the "job descrip-tion."

Now let's start the work of developing your relationship con-tract for a successful relationship with Mr. Right. **The first step is for you to identify your own individual relationship contract (your expectations).** Once you have identified your expectations, then you must decide as to which expectations are most important and which are less important. Part of this process is accepting that you can't have everything you want in a relationship. This means you must ask yourself some really difficult questions. You will have to do some prioritizing of your expectations.

Activity

Why do you want to become a couple? What are your expecta-tions for a relationship? What expectations of yours are important for you to have met by Mr. Right? Be honest about what you expect and write down your thoughts. For example, I want a man who:
• wants to talk about current events
• likes to travel
• has enough money to enjoy fine restaurants
• enjoys going to musical comedies
• wants a monogamous relationship
• prefers staying at home and spending our free time together

Look over your list of expectations. Make sure you have identi-fied what you really want, rather than what you believe you deserve because of your looks, intelligence, age, career, financial status, etc. These are your expectations, and when you date you should deter-mine if this man is able to meet them. If you are honest, any rela-tionship you have has the potential for being successful.

The **second step** is for your Mr. Right to do this activity. Remember that he is also looking for someone who will meet his expectations.

The **third step** is for the two of you to do the next activity together. If you are still single and looking for your Mr. Right, you will, of course, skip the second and third steps. It is important that after finding Mr. Right you both do these two activities.

Activity—with Mr. Right

The two of you share the written expectations for a relationship that you listed in the previous activity.

1. How are your expectations similar?

2. Do you have different expectations for the relationship? If so, talk about these differences.

3. What changes are you willing to make to meet each other's expectations? It is important to be specific, reasonable, fair, honest and genuinely concerned about the relationship. Don't try to force a change on the other, talk about what you're willing to do in the relationship.

4. Which expectations are you unwilling to meet? For example, do either of you have expectations for:
   • having children
   • living separately
   • remaining closeted
   • being monogamous
   • moving to a new location

If you do this activity honestly, your relationship has a greater chance of becoming successful.

It is important to know each other's individual relationship contract before becoming a couple. Clearly discussing both your expectations before becoming a couple would help you have more than just a chance of success. Mr. Right should be someone who can meet your most important expectations and vice versa. Still, it is impossible for you both to know all of each other's expectations when you become a couple. Successful couples, however, do address each other's expectations throughout the entire relationship.

Activity

You and your lover should schedule two days a week for this activity. One of you makes one request on one day and the other makes one request on the other day. You must say you "want" something, for example, "I want you to take a long walk with me," or "I want you to help me decide what night to invite my mother over for dinner with us," or "I want you to give me a back rub." The requests must also be doable that day. This activity helps you ask your lover to meet your expectations. You may want to place conflict areas off limits, such as sex or money. Also, you both must agree in advance to carry out the "want" of the other.

Remember, it is important to acknowledge and accept that Mr. Right is different from you, so his expectations will be different from yours. There is no Mr. Right who will be so similar to you that you will have the same expectations. In fact if you were that similar, the relationship could be quite boring! However, while dating the challenge is to decide whether his expectations are so different that (1) he is really Mr. Wrong or (2) he is really Mr. Right, and his differences are acceptable.

Relationships become successful when both men know and agree to each other's relationship contract: Both men must be honest and must talk about their expectations. The truth isn't always pleasant, but it is what makes our relationships work. There can't be any surprises.

Trust is the foundation for all relationships. Male couples don't always have legal benefits, but our trust can be more permanent than the legal contract nongay couples have obtained.

Christopher and I talked a lot about our relationship contract years before we had our commitment ceremony, but we incorporated those expectations into our vows. We still quote those vows when we are having a disagreement. Christopher's vows to me during our commitment ceremony (his expectations and his promises) are in bold type:

Kenneth, I realize it would be impossible to tell you all the things you mean to me, but you truly are my **playmate, friend** and **soul mate**. I love your jazzy white hair and impish smile Your kind and sweet disposition (and the other part of you that no one else sees). You are there when I need protection and there **to share** my joy and achievements and I love you. I promise **to sing and dance to laugh and have fun with you sharing** all the wonders life has to offer. I promise to share the happiness and try to lessen the sorrows, to build and share our lives together in **symbiosis**, each of us **compensating for skills the other lacks**: my **impulsiveness** and your **retentiveness** my **creativity** and your **logic** and my **chaos** and your **orderliness**. This ring is a symbol of the love we share of **growing together and separately** through all we will do throughout our years together.

And my vows to Christopher (my expectations and my promises) are in bold type.

Christopher, together we have built a unique place together. And in this unique place, we **dance, sing, play, and laugh** with each other and at each other. This place which we have built together is our sandbox. Our sandbox is a place where we can do all of these things—two kids **playing together** in the sand. I want to **spend the rest of my life with you** in our sandbox. I have chosen to do so because you are **sweet, smart, kind, creative, sexy, inquisitive, playful, and passionate**. And most of all, I want to spend my life **laughing** with you. In front of all of our friends, all of whom I consider to be our family, I make a promise to you. I promise to continue to **laugh** and to be **playful.** I also promise (now that you hang your clothes on hangers all facing in the same direction) to be **less compulsive.** I promise to **cherish** you, **support** you, **hold** you, **talk** to and **listen** to you, **trust** you, **honor** you, **comfort** you, and love you for the rest of my life. I will **be there always,** for you as your friend, your lover, and your life partner. I give you this ring as my commitment to this promise.

Of course we have disagreements in our relationship, but they are easier to resolve because we are aware of our relationship contract—our expectations and our promises. For example, Christopher loses things because he puts them away in the most unusual places, and we spend lots of our time together looking for them. But we don't have arguments about these things, because I expect **chaos,** but I laugh at what he has done. **Laughing at him** does upset him; but I did say "laugh…at each other" in our contract. He laughs at me when I remind him about our vows because I did promise to be less **compulsive.** But he still expects this of me.

PROFESSIONAL HELP
My next recommendation may sound a little off-the-wall. In fact it may not make any sense if you are just beginning your relationship with Mr. Right. But **I recommend that you see a qualified relationship therapist some time during the first two years of your relationship.** At present, most male couples only seek out relationship therapy after their relationships have started to fail. It is frequently is too late to save the relationship at that point. Most couples need help at the beginning of the relationship to:

• identify and verbalize their expectations
• help both men clarify what they expect from this relationship
• understand and accept their lover's expectations
• resolve the problems that their expectations may present
• consider the consequences of their expectations

• see if there are any alternative expectations
• develop reasonable expectations for the future

This becomes an easier task with professional help. More male couples than ever are getting this help, but I'm concerned that most do not ask for this help when the relationship is beginning.

Make sure you check the qualifications of your therapist. Almost anyone can legally call himself or herself a relationship therapist, so don't just look in the Yellow Pages for a psychologist, psychiatrist, marriage counselor, therapist, etc. Not all therapists have had experience in working with couples, and most therapists who have worked with couples have not worked with gay men or male couples (and as you probably already know, some therapists are homophobic). Select a therapist who is well recommended and try her or him for a session or two. If either you or your lover have doubts, try another therapist until you are both satisfied.

During the first session, find out about the therapist's training and level of experience with male couples. Don't hesitate to ask questions. Be very clear: You are asking for help in identifying each of your expectations for the relationship. You do not want long-term therapy, you want to work on your expectations. Discuss your concern or complaint with the therapist if you are not getting what you want after four or five sessions.

You and your lover should meet with the therapist together, but at some point you should meet one on one, then together again. As a couple, and as individuals, describe your expectations (hopes, dreams, wants, desires, and fantasies) for the relationship. From this information, the therapist will help both of you identify, clarify, and verbalize these expectations. Do not expect this to happen in a session or two. It will take at least six sessions, plus a lot of talking on your own.

THE CONTRACT MUST BE REVISED OVER THE YEARS

Even if the two of you have continually fulfilled each other's expectations and the relationship is successful, you still have to keep the relationship contract viable. There will be lots of changes over time, some predictable and others that just happen. What we expected from each other and from the relationship may be different one, two, or 20 years after we started dating or had our commitment ceremony.

> Lance and Al have been a couple for 12 years, but 10 years into their relationship they began having "stupid" arguments. Al was frequently irritated over the little things Lance would do—things that never bothered him in the past. Arguments occurred over insignificant things, such as what to have for dinner, what to watch on television, or where to go on vacation. Why were they having a disagreement about food, television, and vacations? They both knew these were "stupid" disagreements and that something was wrong.

When I started writing *Mr. Right Is Out There*, Christopher and I were living in Philadelphia. I was a professor at the University of Pennsylvania and Christopher was an independent artist involved in the larger art community. Together we decided that in order to finish *Mr. Right*, I should take a year's sabbatical from the University and spend it writing the book full-time. We also decided to leave Philadelphia and to spend that year in Florida.

Then the unpredictable happened. We both loved living in Florida and did not want to return to Philadelphia. With much discussion, we made some major changes in our lifestyle. I took early retirement and we built a house in Florida.

Christopher continued working in his studio in our new home, but he no longer had a large community of fellow artists. Since I'm not working we are both at home 24 hours a day, seven days a week. My income has stopped. We added two more dogs to our family. There are few other gay men and even fewer male couples where we live in Florida. Our longtime friends are up north. And to top it off, my mother moved from California to an assisted-living facility to be near us.

There were many changes in our relationship after we moved to Florida, but we were so happy: We had a new home, two new dogs, and lots of free time to enjoy being together. But we began having disagreements that were unfamiliar to us both. We started arguing over "stupid" things.

> **Ken:** "I think you are being too hard on Fauna (one of our new dogs) when you yell at him for peeing on the floor."
>
> **Christopher:** "He keeps doing that over and over. How do you think he's going to learn if I don't yell at him?" (Ken picks up Fauna)
>
> **Ken:** "Well, the only thing he's going to learn from your yelling is to be afraid of you."
>
> **Christopher:** "Why are you holding the dog? He will never learn what is right and what is wrong if you keep rewarding his bad behavior by holding him."
>
> **Ken** (Continuing to hold Fauna): "Who made you the authority on what is right or wrong for the dog?"
>
> **Christopher:** "You're too soft on Fauna. You're going to spoil him, and he will not be trained properly."
>
> **Ken:** "You think you know so much about raising dogs."

We were having arguments with each other that we never had before we moved to Florida. We knew something was wrong. What was really going on between us? What were the disagreements and the arguments about? Certainly the dog wasn't the real issue.

Chapter Five
Being Vulnerable With Mr. Right

In the beginning of your relationship with Mr. Right, everything is just the way you want it to be—lots of romance, excitement, fun, and sex. There are few disagreements, even fewer arguments, and rarely a fight. Then the arguments start and you realize you are different. The work of accepting each other's differences begins and the arguments become fewer. You make decisions on who is going to do the laundry this week, which one gets the new car, whether to take a vacation to a tropical island or San Francisco, and what to name the new dog. Then the disagreements about more important issues start, such as taking separate vacations or having a sexually open relationships, and you begin the work on your relationship contract.

"I'm Out of Here"
Eventually you start spending a lot of time and energy arguing over silly little things. You frequently disagree on some of the decisions. And sometimes you get hurt and angry and aren't even

sure why. You begin to feel disappointed with each other and with the relationship. You start having repetitive arguments, and the two of you seem to be at war over topics that used to be easy to resolve. Then one of you breaks a promise or a commitment that both of you made; one of you may have an affair. Then one or both of you starts to talk about getting out of your relationship. This is really serious and many relationships end at this point, but yours doesn't have to end.

Most men don't realize it, but all successful couples have gone through these "wars," and some have talked about getting out of their relationships. Even our six successful couples had these "stupid" arguments.

• Al was frequently irritated by the little things Lance would do—things that had never bothered him in the past. Arguments occurred over insignificant things, such as what to have for dinner, what to watch on television, or where to go on vacation.

• After moving to Florida, Christopher and I began having disagreements that were unfamiliar to us, such as training the new puppy. We had raised a dog and a cat without any problems. Why was this new dog creating friction in our lives?

• Ricky's work as a physician kept him in the office 50 or more hours a week. Shawn, having moved to Boston from Chicago to be with Ricky, didn't have many friends and was feeling lonely. Also, being a teacher he had much more free time and looked forward to spending this time with Ricky. One weekend Ricky wanted to visit a close friend from medical school, and Shawn wanted to take a trip with Ricky to Provincetown. The following conversation took place:

Ricky: "I never get to visit with my friends now that we are a couple. I feel like I don't have my own life. I love you and am glad you moved here to Boston, but I don't want to spend so much time together."

Shawn: "I know you work long hours and some Saturdays, but I see so little of you now. I don't like begging and pleading to do things with you, but I really wanted us to go to Provincetown this weekend. I'm really hurt that you would rather spend this weekend with your straight girlfriend from school."

Ricky's complaint was that they saw too much of each other, but Shawn didn't understand that. "What I don't understand is that when we do see each other, it is usually with other people. We rarely go out just by ourselves. I keep wondering what was really going on. I know he loves me. We have almost broken up a couple of times, and then he holds me and says he doesn't want to lose me. But then why doesn't he want to spend time with me? Why doesn't he want to go to Provincetown with me? Why does he push me away and say things that he knows hurts my feelings? I have tried to get him to talk about it. I have asked him what he would like the relationship to be and he doesn't respond. Maybe he is too afraid of saying the wrong thing. I love him to death, but this relationship doesn't seem to be working."

• Jeff and Gary found themselves having arguments in the 1970s when Jeff started socializing with friends at some of the local gay bars. Gary, however, believed the only reason to go to bars was to meet someone for sex. Jeff enjoyed meeting his friends and being cruised by some of the men in the bar, and when he came home he would tell Gary about these men. Gary would then accuse Jeff of wanting to have sex with these men, and an argument would follow. Because of these arguments, Jeff would either stop meeting his friends at the bar or lie about going to them. These two men rarely had disagreements or arguments, but they were having problems now.

• During their early years living together, Glen and Mike had at least one big argument every month about money. Mike would get angry when the credit card bill arrived. He believed Glen was spending too much money. The disagreements continued. One day Glen drove home with a "toy"—his first sports car—and he believed Mike would be equally excited and happy. However, that didn't happen:

Mike: "Glen, we can't afford a sports car. You don't think before you spend money, and you have become a spendthrift."
Glen: "I'm so excited about getting this new car, and we can afford it. Why do you ruin all my fun? I'm really angry that you can't be more supportive."
Mike: "But if you keep spending money like this, we will never have enough money to build our own home."

Glen and Mike's disagreement then escalated into a major argument.

• Ethan and Ryan had an agreement to be monogamous. One day a very attractive man cruised Ethan, and he decided to act on his sexual desire. When Ryan found out about the affair, he was very hurt and angry. There was a very bad argument that almost ended their relationship.

Sadly, most of the disagreements that end our relationships are about something as "stupid" as the argument about training the dog, or spending the weekend in Provincetown, or being late for dinner. Many of these disagreements continue and never seem to get resolved. Sometimes the disagreements escalate into critiques and attacks of each other, and the two men begin to think or say:

• He just doesn't understand me.
• I feel worse after we talk.
• We spend so much time fighting.
• If he really loved me, he wouldn't do all those things that upset me.

• Since we are spending so little time together, he must not enjoy being with me.
• I wish we had more sex.
• I wish he were more affectionate.
• We don't have fun together anymore.
• I don't think he is really Mr. Right.

Then we begin to think, *It would be easier to be single,* or *I want out of this relationship.* Sometimes one of us gets so angry he shouts, "I'm out of here," and then we get scared because we really don't want our relationship to end.

Sometimes we get so scared over our "failing" relationship that many of us go to a therapist claiming "he just doesn't understand me" or "he doesn't love me anymore." And the therapist (who frequently doesn't understand male couples) works with us to improve our "failing" relationship. So we work harder on our relationship, but we still feel angry, hurt, and disappointed, and we may even continue to have constant arguments or another affair, and our relationship isn't much better. Eventually these disagreements become destructive to our relationship.

Why am I feeling so hurt with this man who loves me? Why am I always so angry with him? Why am I feeling disappointed? Why are we fighting with each other? What's wrong with this relationship? What's going on? These questions occur to many of us, and when they do we start thinking about getting out of the relationship. This is a critical point in all of our relationships. And as usual, we have a choice: (1) get out and have another unsuccessful relationship or (2) stay in the relationship and ask ourselves a very important question—**What's going on?**

What's Going On?
You need to look at your **vulnerable self** to find out what is really going on with you and with your relationship. The hurt, disappointment, and anger you are feeling is really an expression of your vulnerability. You feel vulnerable when you believe you are being rejected, abandoned, or neglected; you feel vulnerable

when you feel unloved, powerless, inadequate; and you feel vulnerable when you don't feel valued or respected by your lover. **These are your emotional expectations, and so you feel vulnerable when your emotional needs are not being fulfilled.** Men do not like to feel vulnerable—almost any feeling is easier for us to tolerate than vulnerability. **I believe gay men feel even more vulnerable in our relationships than nongay men because at some level we believe the homophobic myth that our relationships won't last.**

We want our lover to fulfill our emotional expectations, and when he doesn't we feel hurt, angry, and disappointed, such as in these situations:

Ricky: "I never get to see my friends now that we are a couple. I feel like I don't have my own life. I don't want to spend so much time together."

• As you saw in Chapter Two, Ricky had made a promise, "I really understand this (moving to Boston) would be something new for you and that it would be lonely for you. If you move here, I will try to be supportive and helpful."

• In their relationship contract, Ricky was to be "supportive and helpful" when Shawn was feeling lonely.

• Shawn had been feeling lonely, and he expected Ricky to be "supportive" by taking care of him, such as spending the weekend together in Provincetown.

• Shawn became hurt because Ricky was not there for him as he had promised.

• Why wasn't Ricky being supportive? What was going on with Ricky?

Mike: "We can't afford a sports car, you have become a spendthrift."

• Glen was feeling insecure about spending so much money.

• Glen wanted Mike to take care of him by getting excited.

• When Mike didn't get excited, Glen became disappointed and angry.

• Why wasn't Mike being supportive? What was going with Mike?

When our lover doesn't fulfill our emotional expectations and we feel vulnerable, we start behaving like a man is suppose to behave. Think about it. What do you do when you feel vulnerable?

• **You try to get your lover to change.** And when he doesn't you may become seductive, pout, or respond with tears, hoping that this might provoke him to change and do what you had expected he would do in the first place. If he still doesn't respond, you may give him the silent treatment for two or three days.

• **You get angry.** Getting angry is the easiest way to avoid being vulnerable. If you feel vulnerable, you frequently want to strike back at your lover. Your anger gives you back your sense of being in control, and having power in the relationship makes you feel better. Instead of your scary feeling of vulnerability, you are now hurting your lover with your anger.

But all of us know that in behaving like a man, trying to change our lover or getting angry with him, really doesn't work. We can yell, scream, throw things, and give him the silent treatment, but we are still vulnerable. We continue to feel hurt, rejected, neglected, scared, and disappointed. Eventually our vulnerability has caused another relationship to become unsuccessful.

Therefore, you have to have your emotional expectations fulfilled in order to have a successful relationship. You don't want to reach this "vulnerability breaking point" and end your relationship. The message from the previous chapter can't be emphasized enough: Having a successful relationship is based on the fulfillment of mutual expectations. This chapter expands that message. **The goal of this book is to help us develop and maintain a successful relationship with another man. Successful relationships are based on fulfilling both men's expectations, including the emotional ones.**

Identify Your Emotional Expectations

So how do you identify the emotional expectations that may be causing your relationship problems? We have discussed our relationship contract and our expectations. You may have done an excellent job of identifying your expectations, such as where you are going to live, whether to have a joint checking account, who will do which household chores, and whether to make a commitment to monogamy. But emotional expectations are rarely identified or discussed—until there is an affair, a broken promise, an argument, a request for separate vacations, or a midlife crisis.

All of us must (1) become aware of our vulnerabilities and (2) know what we really expect and want emotionally from our lover. We must look beyond our fights and look at our vulnerable selves. You can do this by getting help from a qualified therapist, or **you can do this yourself.**

Use your anger

Instead of using your anger in a negative way, you can use your anger to help your relationship become successful. Getting angry is a way to avoid being vulnerable, so stop, look, and identify what is causing you to be angry. The anger you experience with your lover is really an expression of your hurt, frustration, inadequacy, neglect, or rejection. With your anger you can yell, scream, and throw things. These behaviors may make you feel better temporarily, but your hurt feelings will still be there. You are still feeling vulnerable, and your relationship will suffer.

Anger is like pain—it can be viewed as good and bad. We can express our pain by complaining so much that no one wants to be near us, or we can remain silent and ignore the pain and eventually die from some undiagnosed illness. On the other hand, pain tells us something is wrong and we can go to a physician who will use the pain as a diagnostic tool to find out what is wrong and possibly save our lives.

Both anger and pain tell us that something is wrong and they can become diagnostic tools for male couples. **Men in successful relationships use their anger to identify what is really causing**

problems in their relationship. Many men don't realize the "stupid" disagreement (the dog, managing money, spending time together, being on time, where to go on their vacation, buying a car, decorating their home, etc.) is not what is really going on between them. Have you observed that the conflicts with your lover seem to be about topics that are really not so important and probably won't be remembered in a few weeks? Most men spend their time and energy arguing about those "stupid" topics and ruining their relationships rather than identifying and resolving what is really going on—the fulfillment of their emotional expectations.

In your relationship, do you talk more about your anger than your hurt? Do you get angry and blame your lover for your disappointments? Do you have trouble telling your lover you are feeling neglected? Telling him you are hurt, disappointed, or neglected makes you vulnerable, **but it also helps make your relationship successful.**

Activities

1. Every time you feel angry, write on a piece of paper:
   • the situation prior to feeling angry,
   • the thoughts you were having
   • what they have in common (e.g. fear of criticism, being treated unfairly, being rejected)

2. When you are angry:
   • Ask your lover for some physical closeness, such as putting his arms around you, holding your hand, sitting on your lap, etc.
   • Tell him what is bothering you (he just listens). Be specific.
   • Then tell him what you need to happen to help you feel better right now (which may have nothing to do with him).

3. Audiotape or videotape an argument with your lover, and then review it together.
   • Carefully listen and observe every statement and movement, frequently stopping the tape and discussing what you just saw

and heard.
- Identify what was making you angry that wasn't being said during the argument.
- Discuss what you were arguing about and try to identify what was really going on with you during this argument.

After doing any of these activities, take a walk with your lover. Talk about what you see, your day, and what you would like to do this weekend. But there is just one simple rule during your walk: Problems, conflicts, and the activities you have just done cannot be discussed during this time. This is your time together; it is a chance to reconnect and affirm your love for each other.

ASK YOURSELF, *WHY AM I FEELING DISAPPOINTED?*

When you are experiencing hurt, ask yourself, *What am I disappointed about?* For example, are you disappointed because your lover:

- doesn't take care of you
- doesn't do things for you
- doesn't spend time with you
- wants too much closeness
- takes charge
- wants you to take charge
- leaves you alone
- doesn't leave you alone
- expects you to make decisions
- deserts you
- neglects you
- spends too much time with his friends or family
- doesn't make you feel wanted
- doesn't ask you if you need anything
- disagrees with you
- doesn't change when you ask him to change
- expects you to change
- acts like he doesn't want to be with you

- resists being close
- doesn't want to be affectionate
- doesn't satisfy your sexual needs
- gives you the silent treatment
- never tells you he loves you

LOOK AT YOUR PERSONAL HISTORY

You may not even be aware of your emotional expectations during an argument, and they may not even be related to your present relationship. These emotional expectations or needs could be part of your history. What you experienced with your family while growing up may affect your present relationship. For instance, you could have received the message that all men are bad if your father left your mother and she constantly complained that men couldn't be trusted. Even if she didn't talk about your father's departure, you may have felt abandoned when he left.

When Philip was growing up, his mother always made her needs less important than the needs of her husband. After she died, Philip told himself that his mother was better off dead than being treated as a maid, cook, chauffeur, and call girl by his father.

Philip is now a 33-year-old executive at a major bank. He is a great looking guy who is constantly being cruised, but rarely finds himself interested in any of the men he meets. He is only interested in dating men who are from another country.

Jose was typical of the men Philip dates. Jose was from Spain, a graduate student at a local university, has jet-black hair and dark eyes. After six months, Philip enjoyed being with Jose so much that he asked him to move in with him, even though he knew Jose would be returning to Spain when his student visa expired. When Jose studies ended, Philip decided he was not going to move to Spain with Jose since they had known each other for less than two years.

When Philip started dating again, he went to a party at the International House at the university Jose had attended. He hoped to meet someone as exciting as Jose—and he did. An intense relationship began with Antonio, a student from Italy. Antonio, however, was at the end of the exchange program that had brought him to the university. Therefore, it wasn't long before he returned to Italy.

What is really going on with Philip? Although Philip believed he was genuinely attracted to these men, in reality he was attracted to unavailable men. Growing up, he learned his father was demanding and constantly hurt his mother. So in order not to be hurt, he chose men who could never really become long-term lovers. These men from other countries were never able to hurt Philip like his father had hurt his mother.

After many failed relationships Philip decided to see a therapist, with whom he discussed his expectation that men would hurt him. Philip stayed in therapy for a little less than a year. About six months later, at the same university attended by Jose and Antonio, he met Bill, an English professor. Two years later they are still a couple.

Philip's fear had nothing to do with his relationships. His expectation that men would hurt him came from his past and affected his present relationships. Without realizing it, we learn about men from our parents. I'm not implying that parents cause all the problems we have in our relationships with men, but it is important to be aware that some of your emotional expectations in your present relationship may have their origin in your childhood.

Activity

Write your life story including the joys and pains, your relationships, your family, your dreams and hopes, and your family history. What are your parents' backgrounds? What were their childhoods like? How did their parents treat them? What were your parent's hopes and aspirations, successes and failures? How do your mother and father get along with their siblings and with their parents? What kind of relationship do your parents have?

Under what circumstances were you born? How do you get along with your siblings and parents?

A probing autobiography may help you to identify your vulnerability—your emotional expectations.

ASK YOURSELF SOME QUESTIONS

A therapist can help you identify your emotional expectations by asking you many different questions. The purpose of these questions is to get you to start thinking, feeling, and understanding your own needs. You can also ask yourself questions, which may help you to identify your emotional expectations without the help of a therapist.

- How dependent would you like to be on your lover? Independent?
- How dependent do you want your lover to be on you? Independent?
- Who does the decision making in your relationship? If your lover does, why? If you do, why?
- How close do you want to be with your lover?
- How close do you want him to be to you?
- How much do you want to include your lover in what you do?
- How do you put distance between the two of you?
- Which of your lover's interests bother you?
- Why does it upset you if your lover gets involved in matters that exclude you?
- How do you handle power in your relationship? How does your lover?
- What do you regard as power in your relationship?
- What causes power struggles between the two of you?
- How do you feel about being in charge? How do you feel when your lover is in charge?
- How much do you want to be in charge in the relationship?
- What would it be like for you to have a lover who is your equal?
- How will you respond to your lover when he is ill, anxious, depressed?
- How do you express your love to your lover? How does he express his love to you?

• When do you fear being abandoned? Rejected?
• What would your life be like if your lover "belonged" to you?
• What would your life be like if your lover was possessive of you?
• How does making significant decisions make you feel?
• How much orderliness do you want in your life? Chaos?
• What would it be like for you to give up your independence in your relationship?
• When do you feel lonely in your relationship?
• How does your lover make you happy?
• What would your life be like if your relationship ended?

Gary knew the constant arguments with Jeff about going to the local gay bars to socialize with friends would eventually drive Jeff away, and he didn't want this to happen. Gary really wanted his relationship to work. He decided he had to do something about his anger, and he asked himself:

• *What am I angry about?*
• I'm angry that Jeff spends time at these bars.
• *Why does that bother me?*
• I worry that he will meet someone else, have sex with him, and end his relationship with me.
• *What can I do about my fear?*
• I can tell Jeff and see what we can work out together.

Gary expected to feel secure in his relationship with Jeff and to not feel worried that Jeff would have sex with someone else.

In successful relationships there is a feeling of security—neither lover fearing abandonment. For Gary to identify that he is scared that Jeff might meet someone else, have sex, and leave the relationship isn't enough. This fear of his must be addressed with Jeff.

Gary: "I'm sorry about getting angry whenever you go to the bars with friends, but it scares me that you might meet someone for sex and end our relationship."

Jeff: "I'm glad you told me my going out scared you. I didn't know what was going with you, but I now understand. You know I love you very much, I'm not going to ever have sex with anyone else, and I'm I never going to get out of this relationship. I would, however, like you to come to the bars with me and socialize with our friends in order to see for yourself that nothing sexual is going on."

Gary: "I've known you wanted me to come with you; I just never wanted to do that. But I will start coming. I think it is important that we go out together."

Gary's emotional expectations had been addressed and the arguments stopped.

EIGHT STEPS FOR FULFILLING OUR EMOTIONAL EXPECTATIONS

When our lover is feeling vulnerable because he is hurt, disappointed, or angry, I really believe most of us have a fairly good idea what is going on, but we don't do anything about it. If this is true for you, ask yourself, *Why haven't I asked him what's going on?* Is it your fear of closeness or your need to be in charge? Or do you really not know what to do? Luckily, his emotional expectations can sometimes be fulfilled by a simple change in your behavior.

Whenever I hear Chris getting angry and I don't know why, I look for the hurt little boy that I know exists behind his mean comment. I know he really loves me and wouldn't intentionally be mean to me, so he must be hurt about something that has or hasn't happened. A simple hug and an empathetic comment is all that is usually necessary for him to let the anger go and to let me know what is going on with him or with us.

Sometimes a simple change in behavior, such as a hug and an empathetic comment, doesn't help. Then it's time to start using the following eight steps for fulfilling your emotional expectations.

STEP 1: STOP TALKING ABOUT "STUPID" TOPICS

It's critical for the two of you **not** to talk about the topics that precipitate arguments, such as which one of you is going to discipline the dog, wanting a weekend in Provincetown, or buying a new sports car. These topics may seem important today, but having a successful relationship is much more important than "stupid" topics. Think about it:

- Do you talk about who is going to discipline the dog more than you do about your insecurities?
- Do you talk about spending the weekend in Provincetown rather than your loneliness?
- Do you find it easier to be silent than to say, "I'm really afraid," when your lover didn't get excited about your new car?

If your lover had known your emotional expectations or if you had known his, the argument between the two of you would be quite different. For a successful relationship, you both must talk about your emotional expectations.

In Florida many of our new friends were older than us. When Christopher and I socialized with them, the conversation was about their health, estate planning, and wills. Then Richard, our oldest and dearest friend, died.

Before moving to Florida, Christopher and I had talked a lot about retirement and how that would change our lifestyle. We had not talked, however, about our age difference and what that would mean for us as a couple. We certainly had never talked about death and what that would mean for the two of us.

In our relationship, Christopher knew I have always been capable of taking care of both him and me (his expectation). But what about when I become "really old?" Will I be able to meet Christopher's expectations of being there for him (Remember my commitment vows)?

"I promise to cherish you, **support** you, hold you, talk to and listen to you, trust you, honor you, **comfort** you, and love you for the rest of my life. I will **be there always** for you as your friend, your lover, and your life partner."

As we talked about Richard's death, Christopher started to verbalize his fear that I wouldn't always be there for him. I may get sick, I will probably die before him, and he will be left alone. He said this frightened him. I then started verbalizing something that was deep inside me: My fear that Christopher will find a younger lover and abandon me when I get really old (my expectation is that we will be a couple until "death do us part.")

We started to talk about his fear, my fear, and our fears. We both raised many issues. Can our fears be resolved? You bet they can, because we want to resolve them. We talked more and more, and we looked at our expectations. We made plans. I took out long-term health insurance. I stopped teasing him about our age difference. He stopped talking about the cute male nurses he would hire to take care of me if I broke my hip. We reaffirmed our love for each other.

After this conversation, we stopped having disagreements that didn't make sense, such as the one we had about training the new puppy (but I still think Fauna is well behaved and doesn't need to be disciplined—but maybe I'm wrong).

STEP 2: STOP USING ANGER TO AVOID BEING VULNERABLE

It's unrealistic to believe you will never be angry with your lover or that he will never be angry with you. However, constant arguments and fighting can destroy your relationship. It isn't the topic that's destroying your relationship, it's your attempts to avoid being vulnerable. You avoid being vulnerable by:

• expressing your anger, such as blaming your lover, attacking your lover with criticism and sarcastic comments ("You are so fucking stupid.")

• remaining silent and withdrawing from the situation. Keeping anger bottled up inside, however, will not only ruin your relationship, it can also cause low self-esteem, ulcers, alcoholism, depression, and heart attacks.

It is important for you and for your lover to stop denying and avoiding your vulnerability. Instead, use your vulnerability to identify your emotional expectations. Everyone has emotional expectations, and not having these expectations fulfilled causes real big problems for the couple. Additionally, when your emotional expectations are not fulfilled, you will feel hurt, angry, and disappointed.

STEP 3: ON SOME OCCASIONS
YOU MAY NEED A "BITCH SESSION"

Ryan was very hurt and angry when Ethan broke his agreement by having an affair. They had a huge fight and almost ended their relationship. It was difficult for Ethan and Ryan to communicate because of Ryan's anger. Ryan knew anger is dangerous to the relationship and can be viewed as an attack, but he needed to get a lot off his chest—he needed a "bitch session."

I know I said earlier that expressing your anger could destroy your relationship, but if the anger is so intense that it is impossible to have a discussion, schedule a "bitch session." **A "bitch session" is a mutually agreed time when only one of you can let his anger out.** However, there must be a time limit (make it short). In Ethan's and Ryan's "bitch session," only Ryan could say anything. It was painful for Ethan to just sit and listen, but they both knew he was viewed as the villain in this situation.

Warning: Do not attempt to have a "bitch session" if either one of you is experiencing rage

There are some angry behaviors, such as attacking or a threatening your lover, that are just not acceptable during a "bitch session." Anger frequently comes out as rage after it has been "bottled up," but there is a difference between anger and rage. Rage is hitting your lover, breaking things, and kicking the dog. Rage is explosive anger.

You can never predict what men will do with their rage. Rage frightens most of us, it is meant to hurt, and it is dangerous. So if your lover threatens you or attacks you—**don't have this bitch session**. The process of addressing your emotional expectations can begin when his rage has been dissipated. Don't stay in the relationship, however, if this guy you love has these rages frequently. Getting out is justified; this guy has serious anger management problems and needs professional help. He is Mr. Wrong.

STEP 4: IDENTIFY YOUR EMOTIONAL EXPECTATIONS

• Your emotional expectations should be identified as your need (problem, issue) by using "I" statements. Now you may be thinking "if my lover had an affair, how can I identify that as my problem (emotional expectation)?" But you are the one who is hurt, and it is your responsibility to acknowledge this by using "I" statements because they are about you and what is important to you. For example:

Ryan: "I'm hurt and want to talk about how my trust has been affected and how that has threatened my relationship with you."

• Do not use "you" statements; they will make him believe he is responsible for your expectations. "You" statements can also be interpreted as an attack or a threat and will only make him defensive. For example:

Ryan: "You are sex crazy. Can't you just go jogging and work out your libido instead of having an affair?"

• The discussion must be about emotional expectations (Ryan expects there will be trust in his relationship with Ethan). The discussion must not be about an interpretation of an event (having an affair is wrong) or about behaviors (monogamy or an affair).

Ryan: "When you told me about your affair, I got very upset and considered getting out of the relationship. We both had promised to remain monogamous." (The emotional expectation has not yet been identified, so the discussion could be around the affair or monogamy).

Ethan: "I know I agreed to being monogamous, but that was when our relationship was just beginning. I think I now want a sexually open relationship."

Ryan: "We can have a discussion at another time about a sexually open relationship, right now I want to talk about our commitment to each other and how threatened I am when a promise is broken. All the trust I have about you and the relationship has been shattered. I feel hopeless and scared. Trust is so important to me."

Now the discussion will not be about a sexually open relationship or monogamy; the discussion will be about keeping a promise and Ryan's lack of trust.

• If the feelings get too intense, stop the discussion and schedule a continuation at a later time. Don't just drop the issue and then have an argument over another "stupid topic" a few weeks later.

STEP 5: LISTEN TO EACH OTHER

Listening is not quite as easy as it sounds. You and your lover need to know what's going on with each of you. This means neither of you is thinking of a response or a defense while the other is speaking. You need to listen carefully to what he says, what he is feeling, and what he did because of what he was feeling. Do not speak, do not defend, do not offer solutions, do not criticize, and certainly don't attack or insult him. This may help you feel better, but this will not help in addressing his emotional expectations.

It takes a lot of concentration to listen and not feel blamed for what he is experiencing. Feeling blamed implies you are feeling attacked, and then neither of you are going to listen to what the other is saying. If you really care about your lover, you will want to know what he has to say and learn what this event really means to him. You need to listen and learn what is going on with the man you love, even if what he is saying seems unjust, exaggerated, and unfair. It will be easier to plan to meet your mutual emotional expectations once you each know you have been heard.

However, even if you are trying to listen, you may not have heard (or don't want to hear) your lover's emotional expectations. The following are examples of you **not** listening:

- You may be threatened by his emotional expectations and may discount them or attack him.
  - "This is bull. What are you really mad about?"
  - "You are making a mountain out of a mole hill."
- "Honey, you're filled with bitterness, aren't you?"
- You may pretend to give in, take the blame, or promise to change when you don't mean it.
  - "I'm sorry, I didn't mean to make fun of you in front of my parents. I won't do it again."
- You may bring up every problem the two of you have had since you became a couple. This is another way to avoid discussing the issue.
  - "I know I made fun of you, but you have also done that to me every time we have gone to my parents home. Then you start complaining the moment we get home about the time I spend on the phone with my friends. I don't know why you can't accept the fact that I have lots of friends."

If Ethan still has not heard Ryan, it is important to bring the conversation back to the issue.

Ryan: "I really want to talk about how my trust has been affected and how that threatens our relationship."

STEP 6: RESPOND WITH EMPATHY

An empathetic response to your lover's emotional expectation indicates you understand, accept, and acknowledge the hurt, insecurity, disappointment, and fears that may be causing his anger. An empathetic response also makes it easier for you to come up with a plan to meet each other's emotional expectations.

Ethan: "I know I can't erase the fact that I had an affair and that you are hurt. I made a promise to you to be monogamous, and I broke that promise. I feel awful because this has hurt you a lot. My relationship with you is so important that I don't want this to cause us to break up. I really want my relationship with you to work. What can I do to rebuild your trust in me?" (Ethan and Ryan's plan to resolve this issue and to meet their mutual emotional expectations is discussed in the next chapter).

STEP 7: MAKE PLANS TO MEET YOUR MUTUAL EMOTIONAL EXPECTATIONS

• Both of you should present plans for resolving the issue. Don't present your plan as the ideal solution; be tentative and honestly welcome his plan. Nevertheless, clearly state the reasons for the plan you are proposing. Make it obvious that you have considered his expectations as well as your expectations.

• Each of you should discuss the pros and cons of each plan as well as what you would do to improve on each plan. This shows your flexibility. If he seems unhappy with your plan, ask: "What would you suggest if you were me?" or "What don't you like about this plan?"

• Then try to integrate the best of both plans, which will maximize the desired outcome for both of you.

• Consider the pros and cons of the integrated plan. Do this cooperatively without either of you dominating the process. No possible solution will completely satisfy both of you, but you can be equally satisfied. It takes time to achieve this balance and still have a winning solution. Keep in mind that your relationship is what is important.

• You both must agree on final plan, and it must become part of your relationship contract.

LANCE AND AL'S PLAN

As we saw in Chapter Four, Al was frequently irritated at the little things that Lance would do—things that never bothered him in the past. Arguments occurred over insignificant issues, such as what to have for dinner, what to watch on television, or where to go on vacation. They both knew these were "stupid" disagreements and that something was wrong. What was really going on between them?

Lance and Al continued to be members of the church where they met each other. Most of their many friends, both gay and nongay are members of this same church. Their social life was with these friends—dinners, vacations, playing cards, and talking on the phone. The conversation was frequently about finances and planning for the future, such as saving to send the children to college and about buying a second home. Lance talked a lot about building their "dream home" in Arizona. Al was usually silent during these discussions.

One evening they had a tremendous argument about a transatlantic cruise that Lance wanted to take. Al claimed they couldn't afford it. (With Lance being a lawyer and Al an interior designer, money was not really an issue; taking a transatlantic cruise was a "stupid" argument.) About an hour into the argument Al started crying, claiming the relationship was over. Lance got frightened and asked him what was going on.

After much discussion, Al talked about his dream (expectation) of always wanting to have children. Lance never knew this. Al began talking about his life being "meaningless"—filled with material things, but nothing to pass on to the future. He was also concerned about being in a job that had become boring. Lance was able to empathize as well as to verbalize that he hoped they could make some changes, but he also verbalized that he didn't want to have children.

Al: "I understand you don't want children, you've always said that. That's why I never mentioned to you before that I really would like to have children. I get really sad when I'm with our friends who talk about their kids."

Lance: "You've mentioned being upset about two things, children and your job. Are these related in some way?"

Al: "I'm upset that my life seems meaningless and isn't going anywhere."

Lance: "I want us to do something about this. I don't want you to feel sad and upset. We have enough money saved, and I have a good income. I think you should quit your job and look for something that you would find more rewarding. I don't know what to suggest, however, about us having children."

Two years later, they celebrated Al's new elementary education degree, his appointment as a teacher in a local school, and their 12 years as a couple.

RICKY AND SHAWN'S PLAN

Ricky's work as a physician kept him in the office 50 or more hours a week. Shawn, having moved to Boston from Chicago, didn't have many friends and was feeling lonely. He wanted to spend more of his free time with Ricky. Ricky, however, stated very clearly, "I don't want to spend so much time together." Shawn responded that this hurt him.

Shawn thought about getting out of the relationship and moving back to Chicago. Rather than take such a drastic step, however, he talked with a friend who was a counselor at the school where he taught. "We have almost broken up a couple of times, and then he holds me and says he doesn't want to lose me. But then why doesn't he want to spend time with me when I'm feeling so lonely? He did promise he would be supportive if I would move to Boston. Why doesn't he want to go to Provincetown with me? Why does he push me away and say things that he knows hurt my feelings? I have tried to get him to talk about it, I have asked him how he would like the relationship to be changed, and he doesn't respond. Maybe he is too afraid of saying the wrong thing. I just don't know what to do. I love him to death and want this relationship to work." His friend recommended that he talk some more with Ricky. **Shawn:** "What I don't understand is that when we do see each other, it is usually with other people. We rarely go out just by ourselves. I keep wondering what is really going on? I know you love me." (The issue is not yet clearly identified.) **Ricky:** "You don't want to go out with our friends anymore?"

Shawn: "It's not that I don't want to be with our friends. I'm really upset that I moved here from Chicago and it seems you don't want to be with me. I want to spend more of our time together—just the two of us. I'm very lonely."

Ricky: "You are lonely living here in Boston." (The issue of loneliness can now be discussed and not the issue of going out with friends.)

Shawn: "To be truthful I'm lonely, but I could do things with some of the other teachers. But I would feel neglected because I wasn't going out with you. I keep thinking you have lost interest in me. What I do then is get clingy in order to get some reassurance that you still want to be in a relationship with me."

Ricky: "I start to pull away when I feel someone is dependent on me. I just realized that's what I'm doing. I view your behavior as dependence."

Shawn: "Oh, my God. I have been doing things that push you away, which makes me even more clingy. Maybe I'm too dependent. I don't like that."

They finally agreed that Shawn would start planning more activities with some of the other teachers and that they would make plans to go away together one weekend a month.

STEP 8: TERMINATION OF THE RELATIONSHIP CONTRACT

I believe the resolution of any issue should also include those behaviors that are so completely unacceptable that trust would be completely destroyed. If one of you does the unacceptable, he knows he has broken the trust and he should know the consequences, including that his lover may choose to leave the relationship. It is important to be able to forgive your lover for a minor violation of your relationship contract, but repeated violations may not be forgiven.

Activity

Identify what your lover could do that is so unacceptable that you would choose to leave him. These unacceptable behaviors should become a part of your relationship contract.

Ending the Relationship

With repeated violations of the relationship contract, you may decide to leave the relationship. At this point, seeing a therapist can help you to admit the relationship is dead and get on with your life. Even if you saw it coming or made it happen yourself, you may find yourself unprepared for the initial impact of your breakup. Suddenly you're no longer part of a couple and everything around you—your home, your favorite music, and your friends—may seem connected to your ex.

Things you took for granted yesterday may have changed today. You may struggle financially. Many of your dreams and plans for the future, as well as your day-to-day experiences, will suddenly be different. And you're faced with being single—again. It's hard to deal with so many changes all at once.

Most of us who have been deeply hurt by a breakup know that little can be done about the pain during the first several days or weeks. Your moods may change daily; one day you may feel "free," the next day anxious and then depressed. But more than likely, you will experience the following reactions to your breakup:

• **Anger**: Although it's important to acknowledge your feelings of anger in the beginning, it's generally best not to act on them. So how do you handle your anger? Try writing letters to your ex—but don't send them. It is best to express your anger with your friends.
• **Loneliness**: It can be very lonely to be without him. You may want to call him, drive by where he is living, or get into another relationship—but don't.
• **Reviewing**: You may spend a lot of time reviewing the relationship, asking yourself: "Why did he stop loving me?" "When did things start to go wrong?" "Could I have done something differently?" This review of the relationship will help you, so take the time to do it.

It will be especially difficult if you discover that your ex already has a new boyfriend. And if you find out "your replacement" seems to be a lot like you, you will probably wonder, "Why didn't he just stick with me?"

You may have various reactions from your friends when they learn about your breakup. Some may be shocked; others may have seen it coming. You may lose some of these friends because they were your ex's friends. Some friends may also be relieved that you're out of the relationship. On the other hand, some of your friends may be angry that your relationship has ended and worry that the same could also happen to them.

Most of your friends will be there for you—and it is essential that you ask them for what you want. Being clear with your friends about what you need is the best way to ensure you get their support. It may be difficult, but you'll be surprised to see how quickly they will find the time to be supportive of your needs. In fact, many friends whom you haven't contacted for months may even call.

Your family might react to the news of your breakup in different ways. They may be very happy because they saw the problems in your relationship. They may also be sad, having thought of your ex as another son. They may also be another source of support for your needs, even if they had not fully supported your relationship with a man.

How long will it take for you to get over the breakup? There is no set answer to this question. For some men it takes days; for others it takes months or even years. It all depends on the length and nature of the relationship, the way the relationship ended, and the kind of person you are. You may feel pressure from yourself or others to move on and get over it.

You will hear the expression "you need closure" from friends, relatives, and your therapist. Take it from me, **there is no such thing as closure.** Your ex was a part of your life and he will always be a part of your memories. Closure is about mourning the ending of relationship, so you should take the time to mourn the relationship that has just ended. Mourning is an important process that will help to prevent you from finding yourself in the same type of relationship the next time. It's up to you to decide how to mourn. For example, you might:

- see a therapist
- write a letter to yourself that expresses your feelings
- talk with your ex about your feelings
- talk to those friends you trust about your feelings
- spend some time alone thinking about the relationship, i.e., *What went wrong with this relationship? What part did I play in the breakup? What could I have done differently?*
- go to a place that was significant to you and your ex and experience the relationship again
- review photo albums, scrapbooks, and video tapes
- see the movies and listen to the music the two of you enjoyed together

Most important, take time to review your expectations for a relationship and your selection of Mr. Right. Was your ex capable of fulfilling your expectations? Were you capable of fulfilling his? Do your expectations make you so needy that no one could ever fulfill them? Do you have problems with emotional intimacy that prevent you from fulfilling any future Mr. Right's expectations?

This mourning process is a good time for you (1) to explore developing more realistic expectations for a future relationship and (2) to examine which expectations of the next Mr. Right you will be willing to meet. This might be difficult, but doing this will improve your chances of becoming part of a successful couple the next time.

Sometimes the mourning process can be overwhelming, so you must also take time to take care of yourself. Be very selfish. Pamper yourself. Go to "expensive" restaurants. Go to the theater. Follow your interests and seek out what makes you happy. During the mourning process:

- Don't make any big decisions.

• Cry when you want to, and don't be concerned about what other people say or think.
• Be with friends who make you laugh and ask them for a lot of hugs.
• Cuddle your dog or cat.
• Call old friends.
• Volunteer at your gay community center.

After you believe you have mourned long enough and have said goodbye to that relationship, you will want to start to go out and see what new men await you. The thought of going out into the "marketplace," checking out men, and getting checked out may make you feel anything from shyness to fear to excitement. Your feelings will indicate how ready you are to start dating. If you can't contemplate going out on a date without feeling scared, you may not be ready—but don't confuse this with the normal "fear" of dating. When you are ready to date, just go out and be your most fabulous self.

At this point, many men start having sex. You might feel excited about hopping into bed with someone new and at the same time you might also feel uncomfortable. Do remember, however, if you start having sex against your better judgment because you're lonely or because you think you should, you may get yourself into physical and emotional trouble. You may find Mr. Wrong and think he is Mr. Right.

Again, I want to emphasize that not all of our relationships end. All of us have disagreements and arguments, but they don't have to end the relationship. It is important that in our relationship, our expectations are met. But as we have seen with our successful couples, and probably in our own life as well—men *expect* to have power, and we often abuse this power by trying to control our lover.

Chapter Six
Giving Up
Control With
Mr. Right

When I came home one day with two new ties, Christopher asked me why I had purchased such ugly-looking ties. My response: "The salesman said they looked so good with the shirt I was wearing." After thinking about it, I realized the salesman was very cute and I hadn't wanted to say no. I wonder how many times I bought something I didn't want because the salesmen were cute.

We give power to influence our behavior, decisions, and feelings to good-looking men; therefore a cute salesman can convince us to buy an ugly tie we don't really want. It also means that many men feel powerful because they are good-looking: expecting to get moved to the front of the line at a gay club, to get invited to parties, have drinks bought for them at bars, and to obtain the best table at a restaurant.

In our interviews with single gay men, Christopher and I asked, "Would you rather be attractive or intelligent?" An amazing percentage said attractive, confirming our belief that gay men give power to good-looking men.

Giving and assuming power started for us as boys. In school, we knew who had the power: the boy who got picked first for sports, the star of the football team, the one who was elected class president, had the most friends, or got more invitations to parties. We held contests, competed, and the most powerful boy always won. When we started to drive, we rarely stopped and asked for directions when we got lost. Asking for directions implies we don't know something and the person giving us directions knows more than we do and this makes him more powerful.

As gay men we are not immune to wanting to be powerful. Older gay men feel more powerful to "twinkies." Young gay men feel more powerful to "old queens." Those who own a BMW feel more powerful to those who own a Chevrolet. Those who wear Armani feel more powerful to those who wear J.C. Penny. Urban gay men feel more powerful to those who live in rural areas. We also feel powerful if we have the best lover, using such attributes as:

- good looks
- age (we value youth over maturity)
- money
- certain professions ("I'm dating a doctor!")
- stereotypes (the "surfer dude," the boy next door)
- sexual ability
- masculinity (or femininity)
- an outgoing personality
- intelligence
- great bodies
- large penises (Have you ever met a man who didn't want a bigger penis or a gay man who didn't talk about having sex with a man who had a huge penis?)

There are power differences in our relationships because we give power to these attributes. And as much as we may hate it or deny it, **there will always be power differences in our relationships.**

Activity

Both you and your lover answer the following questions in writing. Your answers might help you both to identify the areas with power differences.

- If all of a sudden I were no longer physically attractive, what is it about me that would make my lover want to stay in this relationship?
- What do you think your lover wrote down as his response to this question?
- What do I value so much in myself that I won't change it for my lover?
- What do you think your lover wrote down as his response to this question?
- What do I like most about my lover?
- What do you think your lover wrote down as his response to this question?

After you finish, talk with each other about the questions and your answers.

Christopher and I asked hundreds of male couples if there were power differences in their relationships. They denied having any power differences because both men worked and decided together who did the laundry, cooked dinner, and did the grocery shopping, owned cars, took care of the pets, and shared expenses. Many of these men even became defensive, as if something was wrong or bad about having a difference in power in their relationships. However, in spite of what these men believed or said to us, we did observe differences in power in all of their relationships. Sometimes the power differences changed day to day, but there were also couples where one of the men always had the power. This chapter is the longest because having a relationship in which there is a power difference between the two men is the norm for male couples; however, having a difference in power doesn't cause problems by itself. **It is the abuse of a difference in power that causes problems and destroys our relationships.**

ABUSING DIFFERENCES IN POWER

Being in a relationship with a powerful man can sound wonderful (nothing like a powerful man to fulfill our fantasies), but this guy can turn into a real bitch when he doesn't get his way. You can't disagree with him, he gets angry if you ask him for help, and he attacks when you give him feedback. The following are examples of how this "powerful man" may abuse his power:

• During an argument, he will do everything to win, including threats, guilt trips, withdrawal, personal attacks, naming friends or relatives who agree with him and disagree with you, and by saying "Take it or leave it" or "I'm out of here."
• He insists his decisions are always right. You have very little input into home furnishings, entertainment, pets, etc. He makes important decisions without checking it out with you, or even if he does check with you and you have expressed your reservations, he goes ahead anyway. He puts guilt trips on you for not being supportive and claims your unhappiness is hurting the relationship.
• He has a bad temper and easily becomes angry. The slightest thing sets him off. He gets annoyed if he has to wait for service in a restaurant, gets stuck behind a slow moving car, or is put on hold while on the phone. He may break objects, punch and kick holes in doors and walls, slams doors, and hangs up on you during a phone conversation. Living with him feels like you are always walking on eggshells.
• He makes degrading comments and constantly criticizes or blames you for any problems in the relationship. You can't do anything right—from what you do around the house, the clothes you wear, how you spend money, and even your sexual ability. He acts like you couldn't exist or survive without him.

Having power differences in our relationship can cause problems when the "powerful man" abuses his power and tries to control you by:

- verbal behaviors: criticizing, name-calling, put-downs, accusing, blaming, or yelling
- defiant behaviors: smoking in the house
- physical behaviors: unwanted grabbing, pinching, hitting, shoving, punching
- using sex: cruising, being seductive
- abusing trust: lying, cheating, breaking promises
- using guilt, intimidation, ultimatums
- rejecting behaviors: rejecting offers to be supportive or helpful
- being disrespectful, interrupting, twisting your words, putting you down, criticizing your family and friends
- being late, not keeping appointments, going out alone and not coming home
- being bossy, making decisions for you, not sharing
- withholding emotions: not expressing feelings, not offering support, not paying attention to your needs
- denying your feelings, having no concern for things that are important to you, blaming problems on you
- self-destructive behaviors like abusing drugs and alcohol, threatening suicide, getting in trouble with the law or at work
- isolating behaviors like making it difficult for you to see friends or relatives and telling you where to go
- harassing you by checking up on you, calling you to see if you are at home, stopping by at work

Having a power difference in our relationship causes problems when he decides to be the "powerless man" (the doormat) and tries to control you by:

- leaving the majority of the responsibilities for you to handle
- being late, missing important appointments, or ignoring household chores

• breaking promises and not following through with agreements
• questioning where you have been and with whom
• checking up on you to see if you really have been where you say you have been
• planning activities that consume your time
• not liking your friends or family ; refusing to socialize with them
• getting angry and sleeping on the couch or packing his suit-case and leaving the house
• denying there are any problems and not telling you what's bothering him
• not sharing his feelings
• attempting to win arguments through silence, crying, or pouting
• constantly being upset by things in his life and not making any changes
• feeling sorry for himself, complaining, and blaming others
• refusing to try to resolve problems or improve the relationship

MEN CONTROL THEIR LOVERS BY BEING RIGHT

When your lover expresses an idea or one you don't agree with, do you immediately start thinking, *How do you know that?* or *Are you sure that's correct?* Or when he does some project, do you say to him, "Did you really balance the check book accurately?" or "How reliably did you measure that?" It's no wonder our lover gets angry when we assume we can handle a problem better than he can. Whether it comes to making the bed, washing the dishes, or being correct in an argument, men in unsuccessful relationships remain in control by spending a lot of time and energy trying to prove they are "correct" or "right" and their lovers are "wrong." A recent survey showed most men would rather be right than happy. Proving each other wrong is the greatest cause for hurt feelings in our relationships. **Men in successful relationships do not try to prove their lovers wrong.**

MEN CONTROL THEIR LOVERS BY TRYING TO WIN

When we were growing up, some of us were raised (or people attempted to raise us) as "jock boys." We were given trucks, G.I. Joes, footballs, etc., and were encouraged to be active and to be involved in rough-and-tumble activities. We were expected to be strong, brave, and aggressive.

My father gave me boxing gloves for my 10th birthday. I think he was trying to make me more of a man. But "I won" because I never used them.

We learned that winning was only one way to play and fighting was the only one way to resolve our disagreements. If we didn't win, we were a sissy, a wimp, or a "fag."

Those of us who weren't raised to be jocks were raised to "nice boys"—we were the "nerds" or the "geeks." We were told never to be selfish, cause any trouble, question people in authority, interrupt, complain, or upset others. We were told to do what adults asked of us and to help those who needed help. Being a "nice boy," however, is still fighting to win, but in a passive way. When we have a disagreement, we give in, become silent, compromise, or ignore the problem in the hope that it will go away. There is nothing more frustrating than having a disagreement with a lover who passively fights to win, such as when he says, "You can do what ever you want, I don't care. I'm going out."

All couples fight, but being in conflict doesn't have to mean that one of us has to "win" and the other one has to "lose." Having a fight also doesn't mean that one of us has to give in or compromise, and it certainly doesn't mean that we should ignore the problem. Fighting this way can easily kill a relationship. **Men in successful relationships do not try to win an argument at the expense of their lover.**

MEN CONTROL THEIR LOVERS BY USING ANGRY BEHAVIORS

In growing up, we also learned how to express our anger from such role models as our parents, sports heroes, movie and TV stars, and our friends. However, we can be very controlling when we express our anger. We are being controlling in our relationships when we express our anger by:

• being a real bitch
• walking out of the room when he disagrees with us

• yelling at him when he is late
• hanging the phone up on him when he says something we don't like

Expressing anger may make you feel better, but the recipient (your lover) of your mean, "bitchy," sarcastic words may feel hurt, betrayed, resentful, and frustrated. Sometimes these feelings may last longer than the remembrances of the "make up." Also, some men are angry with each other so often that they just expect almost every interaction to become a disagreement, and they stop listening and start attacking each other right away.

Expressing anger is not always good for the couple; in fact, expressing anger can be destructive to our relationships. For example:

• "Where the hell were you when I got home from work?" is an attack. Men who are being attacked will usually attack in return. A fight then begins, and this fight could be the one that ends the relationship.
• "If you paid full price for that shirt, then you are dumber than you look," is anger expressed through sarcasm.

Some of us don't believe we express anger in our relationship, but we do! Rather than using words, we express our anger "silently" by:

• sleeping on the sofa when we are hurt
• leaving the house when we are having a disagreement with our lover
• ignoring him
• pouting when disappointed
• giving in to our lover in order to avoid conflicts

But those of us who have been the recipients of the "silent" treatment do know he is trying to control us. And most of the time, we don't even realize how we are being nasty, hurtful, and controlling. And when we ask if something is wrong, the response is, "There's nothing wrong. I'm fine."

Bob and Jim never seem to have any arguments, but they never spend the holidays together. Jim usually states, "I'm not going to discuss Thanksgiving anymore. I'm going out alone."

Jim shows his anger through withdrawal. Withdrawal may make him feel better because he believes the argument has stopped, but Jim is still angry—silently—and he has made the decision about where to spend Thanksgiving. By withdrawing, Jim is in control.

It is important to understand the difference between the feeling of anger and the *behaviors* associated with it, such as yelling, hitting, throwing things, the silent treatment, or pouting. All of us feel anger at some time, but in a relationship, it is the angry behaviors that are destructive:

• John criticizes his lover for being overweight and says he doesn't want to have sex with him until he loses some of those extra pounds—"You look more like a pear every day."
• Angelo pouts whenever his lover is late for dinner.
• Billy is constantly telling his lover, "Don't tell me what to do."
• Jesse whines a lot to his lover and says, "Don't ever leave me."

I have talked with male couples who have wonderful times together. Things between them are great for days, weeks, even months, then their angry behaviors eventually destroy all of that "wonderfulness." **Men in successful relationships do not use angry behaviors.**

BEING IN CONTROL

Over the years of working with male couples, I have categorized a good number of the men who attempt to control their lovers and the relationship. For example:

• The **steam roller**: He controls his lover by "being in charge," i.e. by virtue of his authority, status, masculinity, age, sexual ability, or money. Such a person believes he knows what is right and what his lover should be doing. These men don't take "no" for an answer.

• The **rational**: He controls by knowing all the facts. He uses logic rather than his feelings during arguments, and his plans are carefully worked out so there can be little discussion.

• The **flirt**: He controls his lover by flattery and personal charm. When you are out together, he is always flirting or cruising other men.

• The **manipulator**: He controls the relationship by constantly plotting, conning, pressuring, persuading, seducing, or trying to outwit his lover.

• The **daddy**: He controls by giving his lover what he wants; he is the father his lover never had and fulfills his dreams.

• The **boy toy**: He controls by being a grateful, cuddly child. He gets his lover to do a lot for him.

• The **macho**: He uses "manliness," toughness, and an always-in-charge attitude in order to control his lover.

• The **doormat**: He controls his lover by being helpless, sometimes in powerful ways, such as "Oh, I forgot," "I didn't understand," "I just can't do it by myself," or "That's just the way I am."

Now you may be thinking, "I don't try to control my lover, and my lover doesn't try to control me." However, the following questions may change your mind. A yes answer is an indication you may be trying to control your lover (or he is trying to control you):

• Do you want to have things done your way? Does he want to have things done his way?

• Do you get upset when you don't get your way? Does he get upset when he doesn't get his way?

• Do you believe your lover does things the "wrong way"? Does he think you do things the "wrong way"?

• Are you jealous when someone cruises your lover? Is he jealous when someone cruises you?

• Are you possessive? Is he possessive?

• Do you plan your lover's time? Does he plan your time?
• Are you hard to live with? Is he hard to live with?
• Are you impatient with your lover? Is he impatient with you?
• Do you criticize your lover? Does he criticize you?
• In talking with your lover, do you say "you" more often than "I?" In talking with you, does your lover say "you" more often than "I?"
• Did you agree to have a sexually open relationship because you are older and afraid your younger lover will leave you? Did your lover agree to a sexually open relationship because he didn't want you to end the relationship?
• Do you allow your lover to control your behavior because you believe you love him more than he loves you? Does your lover allow you to control his behavior because he is afraid of losing you?
• Do you make most of the decisions? Does your lover make most of the decisions?
• Do you reject your lover's offer to help? Does he get upset when you offer to help him when he is struggling with a problem?

Activity

In writing, identify:

• Five situations where you have controlled your lover.
• Five situations where your lover has controlled you.
• Why you or he wanted to be in control in these situations.
• What you think would have happened if you or he weren't in control.

BEING IN CHARGE IS NOT THE SAME AS BEING IN CONTROL

There is a difference between controlling your lover and being in charge. You and your lover have probably worked out a list of duties; you might be in charge of taking the garbage out each week and he might be in charge of making the beds. Being in charge is a mutually agreed decision to accomplish certain tasks and is not controlling.

Controlling your lover means using your power to get him to do something he might normally not agree to do.

As we saw in Chapter Three, each lover is the "star" in the area that makes him special. Being the star really means being in charge; it doesn't mean he's in control. One man in the relationship may be in charge of writing all the household checks because he is very organized (the "star" in being organized), while the other may be in charge of decorating their home because he is more creative (the "star" in being creative). One lover may be in charge of planning social events because he has a more outgoing personality (star), and one may be the center of attention at a party, the other in their home.

> Christopher is in charge of all fun activities because he is more spontaneous (he is the star in being a boy) and I'm the star in maturity, so I'm in charge of organizing our checkbook.

Being a "star" (in charge) in different aspects of your relationship does not imply a judgment of good or bad, better or worse. **Men in successful relationships acknowledge and appreciate their lover being in charge (being the star) in certain areas.** Most of us like being in charge. Being in charge is a powerful feeling and we like feeling powerful, therefore we like being in charge—we fix things, we decorate, we cook, we take care of our lover when he is ill, and we plan parties.

> Jeff and Gary began their successful relationship of 50 years when they were in the Navy. Jeff was more powerful since he was an officer and Gary was an enlisted man. This difference in power has continued throughout their 50 years together. When they left the Navy, Jeff returned to his family's business, a chain of stores throughout California. After his father and uncle died, Jeff headed the company. Gary was always interested in politics and worked for the city of Los Angeles, but his homophobic fear of being identified as gay prevented him from ever running for an elected office.

Jeff and Gary always combined their income and used their money for household expenses and for shared goals, hopes, dreams, and plans for the future. They took many trips around the world and had a vacation home. Money was never a problem in their relationship, even though Jeff contributed much more money than Gary did. Money is power, but it wasn't in this relationship.

Jeff loves large parties and prefers dogs while Gary prefers small dinner parties and cats. During all the years living together, there was never an argument or a fight over what kind of dinner or pet to have—they always had at least one cat and entertained with small dinner parties. Gary was always in charge of making household decisions. This was not a problem in their relationship.

HELPING EACH OTHER IS NOT CONTROLLING

Mike works as a legal secretary in a law firm, which recently brought in additional senior partners. There is now much more pressure on the employees, and Mike has started to have a difficult time at work. Each night he arrives home from work exhausted and depressed, but when Glen asks him what's wrong, he responds with, "I had a hard day at the office."

As the weeks pass, Glen waits for Mike to tell him more about what he was experiencing, but his inquiries were only met with silence. Finally, Glen decided he wanted to do more than just sit and wait for Mike to talk about the problem, so he offered to help.

Glen: "I know you're having a hard time with the new partners, and I've been thinking of some things that might help. My mom and dad have invited us to go with them to Hawaii for a week. I really think it would be good for us to get away and to rethink what we can do about you being upset and worried."

Mike's response was not empathetic—it was an angry response:

Mike: "Just leave me alone and stop interfering. You are trying to plan my future and tell me something is wrong at work. Stop trying to take charge."

What was going on with Mike?

• Mike has misinterpreted Glen's support. He believes the offer to help is really Glen trying to take charge, to be in control. Men frequently misinterpret their lovers offer to help as an attempt to be in control.
• Since the offer to help was interpreted this way, Mike rejected Glen's help.
• We are in control when we solve our own problems. Not being in control is viewed as a weakness and not even our lover can see us as weak.
• Staying in control is what men do when we feel vulnerable. Mike was feeling vulnerable at work. He doesn't want to feel vulnerable; he wants to be in control by solving his own problem.

During many of their years together, Glen and Mike had constant disagreements and arguments. The topic was usually about money (or a quiche), but they were really having a conflict over one being in control and the other resenting it. This conflict is present even when one attempts to be supportive of the other.

Unfortunately, we view our lover's offer to help us as his attempt to be in control, and any help would conflict with our expectation to be in control—to "do it alone." It's as if we believe that receiving help makes us less powerful. So we conveniently dismiss our lover's offer of help, we get to solve our problems by ourselves, and we feel more powerful. How sad! **Men in successful relationships offer and accept help from each other.** These men see their lover as their best friend, and they are supportive of each other. If Mike and Glen really knew this, they would have had a different conversation.

Glen: "I know you're having a hard time with the new partners, and I've been thinking of some things that might help. My mom and dad have invited us to go with them to Hawaii for a week. I really think it would be good for us to get away and to rethink what we can do about you being upset and worried."

Mike: "I have been feeling so vulnerable at work. I really believe the new partners want me to resign and are purposefully making it difficult for me. It feels so good to have your support. I would really like to spend some time away from work and to be with you. Let's go to Hawaii with your parents."

GIVE UP BEING CONTROLLING

Nobody likes to be controlled, especially by his lover. **But to some extent, the feeling of being controlled may be inevitable in any relationship between two men.**

This feeling of being controlled in our relationship happens because of our relationship contract with Mr. Right. As long as the promises in our contract are agreed on by both of us ("I will meet your needs for affection, conversation, and support if you meet my needs for sexual fulfillment, recreational companionship, and admiration") and these promises are kept, we are both happy. We start to control when we are not happy, so we have to look at our relationship contract as a way of reducing those behaviors that are harmful to our relationship.

WE NEED A "MUTUAL AGREEMENT"
IN OUR RELATIONSHIP CONTRACT

I recommend that the relationship contract for all male couples have a "mutual agreement" for all decisions; neither of you can make any decisions without the other agreeing. This will require you to do some negotiating with each other to reach an agreement on decisions. Up until now, one of you may have made decisions for the couple or decisions may have been made because one of you believed in "unconditional love"—my lover and I should be able to do whatever we want to do.

As both of you negotiate to have a mutual agreement on decisions, you will learn how those decisions affect each other and your relationship. You will learn your relationship is based on mutual consideration.

At first you will find yourselves frustrated, as you will not always be able to do what you want to do. You may even feel controlled. However, neither one of you is controlling the other because you both have to agree on all decisions. And that's not control; that's thoughtfulness. The only restrictions you will have are those that prevent you from doing what you want to do, but you will be negotiating agreements that are acceptable to you both.

From the beginning of our relationship, Christopher and I have agreed to have a mutual agreement on all decisions. This agreement was very important in the home decorating area— Christopher likes antiques and I like contemporary. In order to prevent conflicts while shopping for furniture, we had to do a lot of negotiating in order to furnish our Florida home. We did get it furnished—it took a whole year—but we both said yes to all the furnishings in our home. We really love how our home looks, but even more important, we didn't have any disagreements (we may have felt controlled, but that's part of being a male couple).

WE NEED TO SHARE OUR EMOTIONAL EXPECTATIONS WITH EACH OTHER

Glen and Mike met through mutual nongay friends. Shortly after meeting they moved in with each other in the same town where they were born and always lived. They also lived close to their respective families. They never discussed their relationship contract or their expectations or assumptions for this relationship.

During their early years together, Mike would get upset every month when the credit card bill arrived. He believed Glen spent too much money. Glen, however, knew they were both making good salaries and did not spend more than they could afford, but he would get angry about Mike's accusations that he was spending too much money. Their monthly arguments went something like:

Mike: "I just saw our credit card statement. I really think you are spending too much money."
Glen: "I'm no worse than you. You keep spending money on those computer games."
Mike: "We don't spend much money on entertainment, so I'm justified in spending on a few things that bring me pleasure."
Glen: "Well, that's what I'm doing. Why can't you just accept the fact that I love shopping and buying things?"
Mike: "Because we won't be able to save enough money to build a house."

Mike and Glen's disagreement seemed to be about managing money, however, the issue was that they were having a conflict over one being in control and the other resenting him for it. Let's look at this couple as they try to resolve their conflict:

- Glen takes responsibility for his problem by using an "I" statement:
  Glen: "I really don't like our monthly arguments over money."
- He then identifies the issue of control causing their conflict:
  Glen: "I love you very much and don't want these constant arguments to continue because they are having a detrimental effect on me and on our relationship. I get angry when I feel controlled, and I know when I get angry I attack and say things to you that I later regret."
- Mike feels attacked and gets defensive:
  Mike: "I also get angry with you when we fight."
- Glen repeats the problem:
  Glen: "We argue a lot about money, but we are really both trying to control each other."
- Mike's response lacks empathy:
  Mike: "That's who I am. I'm tight about money and I prefer to save rather then spend. You keep spending as if there were no tomorrow. If I didn't watch the budget, we would be broke."

Mike and Glen did not resolve the issue of control in their relationship. It continues to be an issue in their relationship, but since they truly love each other, are best friends, and want their relationship to be successful, they eventually came up with a plan to resolve the money issue.

They decided to have "mutual agreement" to any couple decisions, for example where to go on vacations, spend holidays, or on any major purchases. This meant that Glen agreed to ask Mike for "permission" whenever he purchased something they both considered a toy, and if Mike said no, he agreed not to make the purchase. The same mutual agreement applied to Mike spending money on such items as computer games. The interesting thing is that since the agreement, neither one of them said no to any request by the other.

Then about a year later, a man who works with Glen offered to sell him his sports car at a very reasonable price. When Glen talked with Mike about the car and indicated he would love to buy it, Mike said, "No, it is too much money." Glen, however, did buy the car, believing Mike would be equally excited when he saw it. But that didn't happen. Instead, they had a major fight. Mike attacked Glen by calling him a "spendthrift."

They had never had an argument this destructive since they began their relationship. They even considered separating. But the discussion continued for several days because neither one of them wanted that.

Glen: "I feel controlled when I have to ask for permission to spend money."
Mike: "I get upset when you spend money, so I do expect you to honor our agreement about both of us having to agree on decisions. I usually don't say no, but a big expense like a sports car is different than buying a computer game."
Glen: "I know you get upset when I spend a lot of money, and I also get upset over being controlled. What's going on with us that makes us need to try to control each other?"

Mike: "You get upset with my attempt to control you. I also get upset and feel powerless with your spending habits. It's like you are really in control and I'm not."

Both Mike and Glen made a mutually agreeable decision to get professional help—their relationship was too important to them to take the chance that it would become unsuccessful. With the help of a therapist, they looked at their relationship contract. Remember that they had never discussed their expectations or assumptions for this relationship.

Glen's "secret" expectation was for the two of them to move somewhere in the Southwest—New Mexico or Arizona—even though they both had good jobs, loved their parents, and enjoyed being near their lifelong friends. He never shared this expectation because he assumed Mike wanted to continue living in this town.

Mike, on the other hand, talked a lot about his expectation for the two of them to save enough money so they could build their own home (his family was fairly poor and had always lived in small apartments). Mike assumed Glen also wanted to build a home and to continue living in this town.

Based on these two assumptions, both men felt controlled.

• Since Glen loved Mike and didn't want to lose him, he stayed in this town. But he felt controlled because he believed they were living there because Mike wanted to. He also resented that Mike never asked him if he wanted to live somewhere else.
• Mike felt controlled by Glen's spending habits and his not wanting to save money so that they could build a home together.

When we feel controlled by our lover, we feel angry and frequently rebel (with angry behaviors).

• Glen spent money in an effort to avoid feelings of disappointment for not living in Arizona or New Mexico and for feeling trapped in his hometown, even though he knew his spending upset Mike.

It is our angry behaviors that eventually destroy our relationships.

• After Glenn bought the sports car, he interpreted Mike's criticism as lack of support. He got angry because he was sacrificing so much for Mike by continuing to live in the Midwest.
• Because Glen was so angry, he wanted to do less to meet Mike's expectations to have enough money to build their own home.

With the help of their therapist, Mike and Glen made their expectations known to each other. Both began negotiating, without the other making any demands or sacrifices to meet each other's expectations.

WE NEED TO TRUST THAT OUR LOVER WILL
FULFILL OUR EMOTIONAL EXPECTATIONS

When two men become a couple, we believe we have made commitments to each other—promises—to fulfill each other's expectations (our relationship contract). Even though these promises are not usually shared and we may not even be aware of them, we expect these promises to be kept. But what if he breaks his "promise" to always be there for me? What if he meets someone else? Or worse, leaves me? With these fears we feel vulnerable. And being men, when we feel vulnerable we then control in order to protect ourselves.

Since I'm older than Christopher, I *expect* him to be there for me in my old age and I *expect* him to outlive me. So when he becomes sick, I feel scared and vulnerable. So what do I do? I start controlling—I make sure he drinks hot green tea, eats lots of fruit, drinks lots of orange juice, and that he gets plenty of rest. He is usually up and well quickly, but I'm never sure if it's because he is feeling better or just annoyed at my controlling behaviors. But I know I was doing these behaviors because I love him—and I was scared of losing him (or was I scared that he wouldn't be there for me in my old age?)

Following is an e-mail message I received from Darryl regarding his relationship with Russell:

"My lover (Russell) is a very controlling person. He likes to be in charge of everything and he's always telling me what and how to do things. When he gets home from work he looks around the house and asks, "Why didn't you put your things away?" When I cook dinner, he quizzes me on what I have done and then begins to tell me how I should have done it. I can never live up to his standards.

"He is also a very loud person. He raises his voice so that he's yelling when we have a disagreement. I keep asking him not to yell at me, but he ignores me. And when I tell him his yelling really upsets me, he never apologizes. He never admits he's wrong about anything.

"He's always been controlling. He wants to know what I do on my days off. If I tell him I'm going out with friends, he becomes so unpleasant that I usually just stay home. I could understand his jealousy if these were male friends, but most of my friends are women."

While it's true that Russell's controlling behaviors are unacceptable, he behaves this way because he feels vulnerable: He is scared Darryl will leave him. To some extent Russell is aware Darryl is pulling away from him, and he has become even more controlling. Perhaps Darryl would address Russell's vulnerability if he knew his expectations. As we saw in Chapter Two, men do not like feeling vulnerable, and by being controlling we protect ourselves from our own fears:

• fear of losing him
• fear of being too close

- fear of being rejected, humiliated, or abandoned
- fear that he will "ruin" something for us
- fear he will hurt us
- fear of feeling powerless

Being in control helps us to feel safe. If you think about it, it is understandable that some of us try to control our lover when we feel vulnerable.

- In growing up in a homophobic society, being in control (even passively) helped us to "feel safe" in what we viewed as a hostile environment.
- We become controlling in our new relationships because we have been in a number of unsuccessful relationships where we have been hurt. Somehow we believe that being in control will prevent us from being hurt again.

Sadly, we miss out on having a great relationship with this man we love when we are in control. When we give up control we can:

- tell the truth about ourselves and hear the truth from our lover
- give up pretending to be someone we are not
- lower our walls and expose ourselves—our strengths as well as our weaknesses
- share our joys as well as our pain and hurt
- share problems between the two of us as well as our individual problems
- truly become best friends

A successful relationship as a male couple is one where two men become and continue to be best friends. Best friends are connected to each other and truly care about the other's well being. Being best friends is at the core of every successful relationship. Being best friends means giving up control and allowing ourselves to become vulnerable. However, without giving up control we cannot become vulnerable.

Giving up control when you are feeling vulnerable isn't as difficult as it seems. There are two things you can now do when you feel vulnerable or scared:

- **Ask your lover for his support or help.** Asking for his help means you are taking a risk. This means trust is present in your relationship because you trust that he will respond to your request for support or help. Trusting him can be scary, but it is the most important part of a successful relationship. Frequently your lover knows when you are upset or scared, and he may even offer to help.
- **Accept your lover's offer of support or help.** When your lover offers his support or help, accept his offer. His offer does not mean he wants to be in control; this is your interpretation of his offer (remember, you can change your thoughts). There is a different interpretation of his offer: He does love you and really does want to help.

Asking for help and accepting an offer of help would certainly help Darryl and Russell to have a successful relationship.

WE ARE NOW A COUPLE AND NO LONGER SINGLE

When many of us become a couple, we may keep the same expectations we had when we were single. We still think we should be able to do anything we want. Men who have these "single expectations" frequently say to their lover, "If you really loved me, you would know how much it means to me and you'd want me to enjoy myself. After all, if it were you asking, I would say yes." What he is really saying is, "My expectations are more important than your expectations, and you should be willing to give up your expectations so that I'm happy." He is appealing to his lover to give him his way. He wants to do as he pleases even if what he wants to do is certain to make his lover unhappy.

Men who say this don't seem to be aware that they are now a couple, and their Mr. Right may have different expectations. And if his lover says no to his request, he interprets this as being controlling. This is the most common reason that many men believe their lovers are controlling them. However, the truth is these men have not yet given up their "single expectations." **Men in successful relationship do no use this argument.**

Even though Ryan and Ethan had an agreement to be monogamous, Ethan enjoys cruising. When he came home one day and asked for some time alone in the house, Ryan assumed Ethan wanted to have sex with someone he met at the gym. They had a destructive argument with both men saying nasty things to each other. Both began to think of breaking up—which neither one of them really wanted. Both Ryan and Ethan did a lot of talking, finally resolving the crisis and reaffirming their relationship.

But then an attractive man cruised Ethan and this time he decided to act on his sexual attraction, breaking an agreement to be monogamous (breaking an agreement is a very controlling behavior). When Ryan found out about it, he was hurt and angry, but he did not want his relationship to end. After having a "bitch session," they spent a lot of time discussing what was happening:

Ethan: "I know I can't erase the fact that I had an affair and that you are hurt. I made a promise to you to be monogamous and I broke that promise, which is affecting your trust in me. I feel awful because I have hurt you a lot. My relationship with you is so important that I don't want this to cause us to break up. I really want my relationship with you to work. What can I now do to begin to rebuild your trust in me?"

Ryan: "It's hard to trust you when you act like you are still single, going to the gym, wanting time alone in the house, cruising, and now having sex outside of the relationship."

Ethan: "I love you so much, but a part me reacts with panic whenever I get too much closeness. I've had this problem in all my relationships. I then do something to push my lover away." (When they met, Ethan was attracted to Ryan because he was older and, at some level, he "expected" Ryan to be more independent and not want closeness. This expectation, however, was never verbalized.)

Ryan: "I'm not sure I understand. How does that explain you breaking our agreement?"

Ethan: "I feel scared about being close and being a couple. I always thought that being gay meant not having to be mainstream—you know, a house with a white picket fence, a dog, and being monogamous. Sometimes I feel just like my parents."

Ryan: "Sounds like you don't want to be a couple. Am I doing things to make you feel trapped?"

Ethan: "No, that isn't it. You are my perfect lover, and I do want to be with you. I love you and don't want us to separate. I just never knew what you expected from me and I didn't really know what I expected when I became part of a couple. I had all these concerns about being in a relationship that I never discussed with you. I just wish you would feel more secure when I want to do things alone, like going to the gym and being alone in the house."

Ryan and Ethan continued their discussion, realizing that over the years, they rarely talked about what it meant for them to be a couple. They had only talked about the sexual aspects of their relationship, like monogamy versus a sexually open relationship. They began to identify more clearly why they wanted to remain a couple, what both expected from the relationship, and their fears that the relationship wouldn't work out.

If Ethan were single, he would have more "alone" time for himself and to explore his own interests. He would be free to go out when he wanted to and to go where he wanted to go. He could go out cruising and have sex whenever he pleased. He would make his own decisions and wouldn't have to negotiate with Ryan. Ethan frequently felt controlled in a relationship, but he did want to stay with Ryan.

Ryan and Ethan talked about how different they were from each other. They began to realize they didn't have to give up being who "I am" in order to become a "we." That meant accepting each other as they really were. They also talked about their different expectations, but both continued to be scared because they knew they had to rebuild the trust between them.

WE MUST AGREE TO ANY CHANGES IN OUR RELATIONSHIP CONTRACT

Some men are viewed as being controlling when they try to change the expectations in their relationship contract.

Christopher and I have agreed who is in charge of certain "chores." For example, I write all of the checks for our household expenses and balance our checkbook (because I'm the star in being organized). He is in charge of the garden, and he maintains it to make it our "tropical paradise" (because he is the star in being creative). Therefore, because of our agreement, Christopher expects me to do my chore and I expect him to do his chore.

Now let's assume that I get very busy working on this book and I ask Christopher to start writing the checks. He may resent my request because his expectation is that I will write the checks. Christopher may feel obligated to meet my request because he knows I'm working hard on the new book, but he may still believe I'm controlling him because I changed our relationship contract and he is now doing my "chore."

If your lover tells you that you're trying to control him, ask him what he means by that. Don't defend yourself and don't argue with him, but try to find out why he feels this way. Then look at your relationship contract. Have any changes been made that have not been discussed and agreed on by both of you?

Using differences in power to control one another causes many male couples to have constant arguments; this situation usually ends with both men hating each other and leaving the relationship. But it doesn't have to be that way. We can have successful relationships even with differences in power. In order to do this, however, we must stop abusing our power by attempting to control our lover.

SOME AREAS IN WHICH WE ABUSE OUR POWER

The men who have e-mailed me since the publication of *Mr. Right Is Out There* have indicated three areas of power abuse in their relationships: household chores, age, and money.

HOUSEHOLD CHORES

I don't think anyone really likes cleaning toilets, washing dirty clothes, making the bed, or scrubbing the floor, so these chores have the potential of causing conflicts. But it's not really the chores that are causing problems; it's the unresolved control issues between the two men. Following are five examples and five male couples with control issues.

Men frequently behave as if there is a "right" way and a "wrong" way of doing chores.

In their relationship, David agreed to make the bed and do the dishes. However, Sam is constantly remaking the bed "correctly" and reminding David that the dishes should be washed and put away before they go to bed (David prefers to do them in the morning). Sam is very controlling, he believes it is his duty to correct and educate David.

Men may attempt to control their lover by using a difference that they view as powerful, such as age, "being weaker," culture, or money.

After meeting in a grocery store, Philip and Jose found themselves attracted to each other, and eventually moving in together. Jose was a graduate student from Spain and viewed doing household chores as being beneath him. He said this is the "wife's" work and refused to cook, clean, or do the laundry. Jose's father also did not do the household chores because he was the breadwinner, the "man of the house." Since Philip wanted his relationship to work and had learned (wrongly of course) that giving in is what you do when you are in love, he did the household chores and didn't ask Jose to help; nor did he complain. Philip was behaving in his relationship as his mother did with his father.

Activity

Keep a diary, identifying when you say yes to anyone's request when you would rather say no and vice versa.

Other men make no decisions about who is in charge of the various household chores in order to avoid a conflict. They know this discussion could end up in a disagreement and an argument. These men hope the situation will go away, but of course it doesn't.

Tony and John eat out or buy takeout, have someone clean their house, and send all their clothes to the laundry. Tony and John are afraid that trying to decide who will do what will cause an argument and a fight, so they don't have these discussions.

Then there are the men who compromise. That sounds wonderful, but this is just another way to avoid making decisions and avoiding a conflict about control. And it can also be a way for one lover to get his way, but in a subtle way. The objective becomes doing what it takes to be more clever than his lover.

Curtis and Jim couldn't decide who was going to do which household chores, so Curtis came up with a solution: "Together we will write on separate pieces of paper each of the household chores that have to be done. Then we will each select a piece of paper until all the chores have been assigned." They do this once a month.

At times, Jim feels like he is being manipulated into doing chores he would prefer not to be doing. He would prefer to do all the cleaning and none of the shopping or cooking. Jim never disagrees with the process because it seems "fair," but he believes there must be a better way of making decisions.

Some men just get angry when they are not in control. The decision about which one is to do what chore leads to an ugly battle in which one or both men must "get their way" and win at any cost.

Bill and Ralph argue most of the time about which one is going to do which household chore. The laundry often doesn't get done, dishes accumulate, and mealtime is a "fast food experience." When things get too bad, they have a big fight over who is going to do what chores, and then things get done. And it takes another battle to get them done again.

None of these five pairs of men ever became a successful couple.

AGE

Of course there are age differences in nongay couples; the man usually being a couple of years older than the woman. But in male couples, frequently one is more than 10 years older than the other.

The age difference between Christopher and me doesn't seem as great today as it did 17 years ago when we met and Christopher was 20 and I was 40.

These May-December relationships begin the same as any other couple: We meet, we are attracted to each other, we spend time together, and we have sex. We have good conversations along with a lot of affection, we fall in love with each other, and we become a couple. In my work with male couples, those couples who seem the most successful are those who have an age difference. Each lover brings something unique to the relationship. But more importantly, couples with an age difference are less likely to compete with each other, and competition is one of the major problems for two men in a relationship.

Male couples with an age difference have problems the same as any other couple, but they also have these additional problems to deal with:

1. Couples in which the partners are very different in age are frequently confronted with the stereotypical beliefs we have all learned from television, movies, and from our family and friends. I'm sure all of you in a relationship with an older or younger man have heard the same comments Christopher and I have heard over the years:

- Oh, is that your son?
- He married him for his money.
- What does his family think about that?

Christopher and I had a nongay couple and their 6-year-old son to our home for dinner one night. "Where's your mommy?" the boy said to Christopher. At first none of us understood the question, but then we realized the boy thought I was Christopher's father.

The problem for many male couples with an age difference is that we start to believe these stereotypical messages and we begin to question the age difference. Why is he interested in me? What is he after? What does he want? What is going on with me? With him? Then we begin to believe there is something wrong with being in love with a younger or older man and some of us then feel uncomfortable about our relationship.

Although Ethan and Ryan (who have a 15-year age difference between them) hit it off from the day they met at a gay bar, Ryan has been concerned about his age. "From the very beginning I felt uncomfortable about our age difference. But when some of Ethan's friends and some of my friends began making bitchy comments, I began to think about getting out of the relationship. But after 10 years together, I'm really glad I didn't. I love him so very much—and I know he loves me just as much."

2. Friends and relatives can't relate to the younger or older person.

The entire family adores Uncle Leslie. He is invited to every family function and is a central to their lives. Jerry looked forward to introducing Kevin to Uncle Leslie, but their first meeting was a disaster.

Uncle: "Jerry tells me you two will soon be living together."
Kevin: "Yes, I'm moving into his apartment."
Uncle: "What do you do for a living?"
Kevin: "I'm still in school."
Uncle: "How old are you?"
Kevin: "21."
Uncle: "Do you know Jerry is 15 years older than you?"
Kevin: "Yes, but that doesn't make any difference to us."
Uncle: "What could you possibly have in common?"

Jerry finally rescued Kevin, who was feeling very uncomfortable and really didn't want to spend time with Uncle Leslie in the future. This had the potential for creating conflicts for this male couple. Jerry and Kevin could have resolved the situation with Uncle Leslie by avoiding family get-togethers or by Jerry going alone. This was not an acceptable solution. The problem was not that this couple was gay, but the age difference.

One day Kevin invited Uncle Leslie to the opera. He was surprised that someone so young would find the opera enjoyable. Finding a common interest helped, and Kevin and Uncle Leslie have continued going to the opera, and over time became friends.

3. If the older man has children from an earlier marriage, the younger man is frequently younger than these children.

Victor and Lance had been a couple for five years when a major change occurred. Victor's ex-wife was killed in an automobile accident, and his two sons came to live with them. Previously the children only came for holidays and on short vacations. Victor was 50 and Lance was 28 and the boys were

12 (Cory) and 15 (Brett). Problems began almost immediately between Brett and Lance. Lance enforced some of Victor's rules, and one weekend Brett rebelled and ran away. Luckily they found Brett, but both Victor and Lance knew this situation had to be resolved if the four of them were going to become a family.

Victor: "I love all three of you and I want us to become a family."

Brett: "He's not my dad, and I don't have to listen to him."

Victor: "I consider Lance just as much my spouse as your mother was when we were married."

Brett: "He's not much older than I am, so I don't have to do what he tells me to do, and that's that."

Lance: "I'm sorry you feel that way. I was hoping we could become friends. Would it help if you thought of me as a big brother?"

Brett: "No, because you're not my brother, you're Dad's boyfriend."

Lance: "I'm not his boyfriend, I'm his spouse and I love him as much as you do. I was hoping the two of you would love me too."

Victor: "The problem seems to be that you don't like thinking of Lance as another dad. I'd like the four us to work on this together. Perhaps it would help if we wrote the household rules together and then decide who does what. And perhaps we need more time together. You know what, guys, I can take some time off work, shorten my hours, and spend more time with you. How's that?"

There were more conflicts and Brett ran away again, but gradually the four became a family.

4. They are at two different places in their lives.

Ryan is concerned about their age differences when he thinks of the health issues that will arise when he's 65 and Ethan is 50.

I'm concerned about going to a nursing home alone when I'm 80 and Christopher is only 60.

5. It is not the age difference that causes male couples to have problems; it is the control and power issues in their relationship. The younger man frequently puts the older man on a pedestal and sets him up to be his parent, and the older man frequently treats the younger man like a child.

Dick is 45 and Fritz is 30, and they have been a couple for five years—five years of repetitive arguments. Dick always knows "from experience" what needs to be done, and he is constantly giving "advice" to Fritz. Fritz resents Dick's control.

Dick: "I noticed your car hasn't gone in for its checkup in six months. We have nothing scheduled for this weekend. If you'd like, I will make an appointment for you at the dealership."
Fritz: "No, that's not convenient for me. I have work things I'm planning on doing Saturday."
Dick: "But if you don't take the car in, it will affect its warranty."
Fritz: "I don't want to do it this weekend."
Dick: "You keep putting off important things. I really wish you would get more efficient."
Fritz: "There you go again. It's always me who has to change and do things differently. Why don't you change and stop telling me what I should be doing? I'm old enough to make my own decisions."
Dick: "OK, but don't say I didn't warn you."

Dick and Fritz aren't going to be celebrating too many more anniversaries if they keep fighting rather than resolving the issue of power and control in their relationship.

There are other male couples without an age difference who behave as if there is. I refer to these couples as "Big Daddy–Little Boy" couples. There is one issue that Big Daddy–Little Boy couples have in common with older-younger couples: the issue of power and control. For example:

- Big Daddy feels in control when he is giving.
- Big Daddy feels powerful because he has a "trophy."
- Little Boy feels powerful because he is the sole object of Big Daddy's adoration.
- Little Boy feels powerful because he gets a lot of attention from other men (but, in general, he isn't interested in them), and Big Daddy gets jealous.
- Little Boy maintains control by threatening to leave Big Daddy.
- Big Daddy maintains control by threatening to replace Little Boy.

MONEY

Money is an issue for most couples; no matter how much of it they earn or have. There can be problems when you put two men together because men frequently use money in order to establish control in their relationships. It is common in the relationship between two men for one of them to make a higher salary than the other, and this difference can cause problems. The more financially successful lover may make more of the financial decisions and the less financially successful one may feel dependent or guilty because he is contributing less money to the relationship. Do they merge their incomes to resolve this difference? Do they each have their own checking accounts? Does the one who makes more money get to spend more money on himself? Does the one who makes less money pay less of their expenses?

Making the situation worse, financial differences can be reinforced by careers. Long-term couples in different careers might once have had incomes that were reasonably close, but over the years one of them makes much more money than the other does. A teacher may never make more money than his lover, who was an accountant when they met but is now the CEO.

Ricky makes much more money as a physician than Shawn does as a teacher. To share expenses would be a disaster. For example, eating at a restaurant—to share equally might be a burden for Shawn. But to eat at a restaurant that both of them could afford might lead to resentment from Ricky.

We have seen the conflict between Glen and Mike regarding money, which wrongly seemed to be about managing money. Instead, Glen and Mike were having a conflict over control; one was in charge and the other was resenting it.

Then there is the issue of power and control in our sex lives. Those men who have learned to give up control and play with each other continue to have a great sex life beyond the initial couple years of the relationship. In Chapter Seven you will learn what is it about sex that brings us together and then drives us apart.

Chapter Seven
Continuing Great Sex
With Mr. Right

We are sexual beings. As little boys we got erections (looking at that cute boy next door?) and it felt good when we rubbed ourselves "down there." As adolescents we started getting excited when we looked at other boys (remember those high school gym classes?) and some of us even started fooling around with some of these boys. And as adults, sex gives us enormous pleasure and fun.

For some men, sex can be an awful experience. They may feel inadequate, less than desirable, hurt, disappointed, guilty, sinful, rejected, jealous, and angry. Whether sex is pleasurable or awful depends on what we have learned about it. And what we have learned about sex causes some of our relationships to be unsuccessful.

OUR SEXUAL LESSONS
We start to learn about sex at an early age. There were certain programs we couldn't watch on television and movies that we

weren't allowed to see. And our parents were very secretive when we asked questions about anything sexual.

Recently I was at an office-supply store. A close friend and her 15-year-old son were also there. Joyce asked me about our new puppy (our third dog—a tiny Chihuahua that we had brought home a month earlier and named Marriquita). I told her the puppy was feisty, that she "crawled under the sheets in our bed last night and bit my penis with her sharp baby teeth." Joyce and I started laughing. Her son came over and asked why we were laughing. His mother's response was "You are too young to know." At 15 he was too young to know what? I had a penis, the dog bit my penis, or that his mother thought being bit on a penis was funny?

Growing up we heard comments such as "don't play with yourself," "don't use 'dirty' (sexual) words," "don't read 'filthy' (sexual) books," "you can't go to that R-rated movie," and "don't have sex until you are older (or married)." Most of us also learned from our ministers, priests, rabbis, teachers, school counselors, or our parents that sex with another man was sinful, wrong, sick, or not acceptable.

Our "gay sex education" began as we were coming out. We started to look at male pornography (films and magazines) and we learned a lot about sex and what we should look like—young, well built, handsome, with a washboard stomach. We learned about penises—"the bigger the better!" And we also learned about performing sexually:

- Sex will always be a great experience.
- You should always have an orgasm.
- You have to have an erect penis and it should stay hard during the entire experience.
- When you have an orgasm, sound excited.
- Men are always hot and horny.
- Never say no.

Our education continued as we learned more about sex from other gay men (who have now become our teachers):

• Having great sex is important in a relationship.
• Great sex is having an orgasm.
• "Bigger is better" with penises (reaffirming what we had already learned from male pornography).
• Select "hot" looking guys for our Mr. Right.
• See other men as erotic sexual objects.
• Have many sexual partners.
• Most male couples have a sexually open relationship.
• It's time to get out of the relationship when sex becomes boring with your lover.
• It's acceptable to cheat on your lover if you meet a really "hot" number.

And because of all we learned about sex, **we compare:**

• our physical appearance and penis with other men, and we feel "less" if we don't "measure up"
• our lover's appearance and penis with the fabulous bodies and the gigantic penises of male porn stars
• our sexual ability, and we feel inadequate if we haven't had lots of sex partners
• our bodies to younger gay men, and in comparison we are more wrinkled (this happens as we grow older), heavier, and not as attractive (who is, compared to a 20-year-old?)
• our "horniness"—and not too many of us are as horny as the men we have heard about and read about (remember, most men lie when it comes to their sex lives).

Because of all these lessons about sex, **we question:**

• Will I measure up?
• Will I be able to perform?
• Will I get an erection?

• Will he find me attractive?
• Who is on top, bottom, or on his side?
• Who does what?
• Who starts doing what?

Because of all these lessons about sex, **we feel:**

• hurt when other guys don't find us attractive
• inadequate when we don't have a date
• disappointed when we are rejected
• jealous when our lover cruises
• angry when our lover has an affair
• devastated when our lover of 15 years leaves us for a better-looking guy

Because of all we have learned about sex, (as we saw in Chapter Six) **we assume power and give power to:**

• age (we value youth over maturity)
• sexual ability (we choose a lover because he is great in bed)
• masculinity (or femininity)
• good looks
• great bodies
• "gigantic" penises

And because of all of these different lessons, it's certainly understandable that we have many different expectations when it comes to sex. **And it is these different expectations about sex that cause individual problems for us as well as in our relationship with Mr. Right.**

Our Expectations About Sex

While dating

On our first date with a man, we have learned what to expect and how to behave, and our problems begin.

Ricky and Shawn met 15 years ago on a gay cruise to the Caribbean. They met at the pool, liked each other, and tried hard to please and impress the other. After a fun day at the pool and a romantic dinner, Ricky asked Shawn to spend the night in his cabin. Shawn agreed. However, after a long day at sea, both men had sunburns, had plans to get up early in the morning to join friends shopping in St. Thomas, and were very tired. Neither was horny, and each of them just wanted to go to bed— alone. The truth was that both men would rather have gone to their own cabin and set aside the next night for having sex for the first time. But they both had learned they were expected to be horny and that they should give that impression.

Since neither believed he could say "let's wait," Ricky and Shawn spent the night together and had sex. They said what was expected to each other: "You are fantastic," "Yes, I came," "You are great sex," "You have a great body," and so on. But during sex they were thinking: "I'm too tired to come," "I'm so sunburned," "I hope he doesn't think I'm not interested," "I can't keep this up, I hope he comes soon," "My God, he wants more!" and so on. They both had an orgasm, told each other how wonderful it was (while hoping the other was ready to go to sleep), and struggled to be affectionate. The experience was much less satisfying than it could have been if they had waited 24 hours. They did what they thought was expected, but they weren't honest. By pretending, they set a high sexual standard for the remainder of the cruise.

Many of us believe we have met the "man of our dreams" after the first few dates, and we start to fantasize about becoming a couple. But our fantasy usually doesn't come true:

- He stops calling.
- He avoids us.
- He says, "Let's just be friends."

We begin to think all gay men are jerks or we start to believe the homophobic myth that our relationships just don't work. The truth is that **many of our relationships do end after three or four dates because the man we are dating has had different learning and has different expectations about sex and relationships.** For example:

- You've had great times with him and he has told you how much he enjoyed being with you. But you don't have his phone number, are not sure where he lives or where he works, and he is not always available. These men have learned that sex with another man is wrong, disgusting, and sinful—they are very homophobic and make for a "lousy" relationship. These men are usually closeted and secretive—they may even have a wife and children. They feel guilty after having sex with you. Still, most of us have had a few dates with these men.

- He's great sex—it was fun, enjoyable, and an adventure. He stops returning your phone calls after a few dates, and you rarely see him again. Or, if you do accidentally see him again, he acts as if he has never met you before. These men have learned that sex is for physical gratification. Sex is not a sign of commitment, not a show of love, and not an indication of any continuing emotional involvement—you are just another "trick" added to his list of conquests. These men prefer short relationships or one-night stands. They have separated sex from love and they don't pretend to be in love in order to have sex. They are, however, great sex partners—if that's what you want.

- He's told you how attractive and sexy you are, and how much he really likes you, but after a few dates he says, "I really like you and hope we can continue seeing each other, but I just want us be friends." These men have learned that intimacy can be painful and they don't form long-term, intimate relationships. There is a possibility of a good friendship developing, but there are no guarantees that love will happen. These are the men who "break your heart" because you really thought the relationship was going somewhere.

• During sex for the first time he tells you how much he loves you. Sexual attraction begins at first sight for these men and they fall in love with you from the very beginning of the relationship. They have learned that sexual attraction means "I love you, and because I love you I want to have a relationship with you." A relationship with these men doesn't last very long—a couple of years at the most. After a few relationships with these men you begin to start thinking "I'm going to stay single. Gay men just can't form a relationship."

• Then there are the men who have learned that sex means "I find you attractive, I want to spend time with you, have good conversations, and I want to get to know you." Some of these men have sex with you on the first date, others wait to have sex until they get to know you. At some point, however, these men "fall in love" and eventually become a male couple—but they do not equate sex with love. As a couple, they call their lover their best friend. I believe these men make the best "Mr. Rights" and have the greatest potential for forming successful relationships.

After meeting, Lance and Al started going out to dinner and movies, went to church, and spent a lot of time having conversations. They both knew they wanted to get to know each other before having sex, and they dated for several weeks before spending their first night together.

All of these men have learned a different message about sex and have different expectations for having it. **Dating a man who has different expectations for sex than you have can cause problems,** even if you have been perfectly clear about what sex means for you. He may:

• be clueless about his expectations
• not have been clear with you about his expectations
• not have been honest, or
• you may have heard what you wanted to hear

Of course our expectations about sex may also change over time. For some men sex may just be fun, and then later it may mean "I like you," then "I love you," and finally a relationship. You must decide for yourself what sex means for you.

My "formal" sex education as a child was very limited. My father (who erroneously assumed I was nongay and that I was going to have sex with women) gave me a very simple message—"don't marry her if you have sex with her on the first date."

So I went off to college, met this wonderful guy, and had a date with him. My friends all said if you like him, go ahead and have sex. So we had sex on the very first date, and I never heard from him again. I learned my father was right and my friends were wrong—do not have sex on the first date. I never did it again!

The men you date may try to influence you, but only you should decide which of the many expectations for sex is best for you. All are acceptable choices and each has its pros and cons, but not all expectations lead to a successful relationship with Mr. Right.

WITH MR. RIGHT

Eventually after all the trials and tribulations of going out, dating, having sex, and exploring our mutual expectations and interests, we finally meet Mr. Right and become a couple. Our expectations for the first few months are to enjoy spending time with each other and having lots of great sex. We also expect that our sex life with each other will continue to be just as great. However, this is not true. **Changes do occur in the sex life of most couples:**

• Sex can become routine, predictable, boring, and infrequent.
• Our sexual interest in each other may decline.
• One or both of us may have difficulty getting an erection.
• One or both of us may lose our interest in sex as we age.

In our talks with male couples who had been together for more than five years, Christopher and I asked them, "What bothers you most about your sex life?" Their biggest complaints were:

- We don't cuddle enough.
- We only kiss during sex.
- Sex has become routine—the same time, place, and the same way.
- We don't have it often enough.

And over the years as our sex lives change, we make decisions based on our expectations. For example, some men:

- Expect sex to become less important (less interesting, less passionate) as they age (or as their relationship matures), so they stop having sex with each other.
- Expect sex to become boring (routine, predictable) with their lover, so they convince each other to have a threesome.
- Expect sexual problems (not getting an erection, have trouble with their orgasms—coming too quickly or taking too long), so they decide this is "normal" and don't do anything to correct the situation.

What's interesting is that many men believe these changes are "normal," so they spend little time communicating with each other about these changes and their expectations. They also do not take the time to try to find new and different sexual behaviors to improve their sex life with each other. However, these are the same men who do manage to find the time to cruise, have affairs, have a sexually open relationship, and to start the process all over again. These men have *learned* they will have a great sex life again with a new lover. These are the men who have also *learned* that having great sex is the most important part of a relationship. But guess what—these men just don't get it. **Men in successful relationships have learned that great sex is important, but great sex is more than having an orgasm: It is about sharing with each other, being** romantic, communicating likes and dislikes, experimenting with new sexual behaviors, and having fun with each other.

In all reality, sex with a long-term lover can become boring, and the excitement may decline. Other changes may also occur—you might have some difficulty getting an erection, not have an orgasm every time, and not want sex every day. However, it doesn't have to be that way. **Men in successful relationships do something to continue having an exciting sex life with each other.** The following seven suggestions can help:

1. COMMUNICATE YOUR SEXUAL EXPECTATIONS

You have to be honest, open, and direct with your lover. Both of you have to let the other know what:

- feels good and what doesn't
- sexual acts are exciting and unexciting
- you want to happen before, during, and after having sex
- sexual behaviors you want to try that are different and new

2. USE AN "I" STATEMENT TO EXPRESS YOUR EXPECTATIONS

- "I want you to talk dirty to me during sex tonight."
- "I want you to use more tongue action during oral sex."

3. COMMUNICATING DOESN'T ALWAYS MEAN YOU HAVE TO USE WORDS

Sometimes it is better to show him how to do something, rather than trying to tell him. Show him how you like to be masturbated, have oral or anal sex, or any other sexual behavior.

4. AVOID BLAMING HIM IF YOU AREN'T GETTING WHAT YOU WANT

- "I might have come if you had done a better job."
- "If you loved me, you'd take more time, whisper sweet nothings in my ear, and massage my back."
- "If you wanted to get me excited, you'd play with my penis more."
- "You never want sex. You must be getting old."

5. TRY NEW SEXUAL BEHAVIORS

Many male couples seldom try anything new. What would happen if you saw the same movie over and over? You would probably get bored and not want to see it again. The same is true for sex. Doing the same behaviors over and over again can get boring. **Men in successful relationships try new sexual behaviors**, such as:

• Being seductive, wearing sexy outfits that turn him on (if you don't know what turns him on, ask him).

Ricky and Shawn are embarrassed to go to places that sell sexy clothes; however, they did find places on the Internet. Ricky wears a leather thong, which really gets Shawn excited. They also buy various sex toys and continually experiment with new behaviors.

• Being together in a hot tub or a shower are great ways to get excited. Gently exploring each other's bodies can be a really exciting. Try to discover which parts of your bodies are the most sensitive. You might be surprised to discover the penis is not the most sensitive part of the anatomy.
• Taking control. If one of you likes to be in control in your relationship, this can be used to create sexual excitement through role playing various scenes.

Both Glen and Mike acknowledge they have an issue with wanting to be in control. They have used this in their sex life with each other. They role-play during sex, such as "master" and "slave," policeman and thief, prison warden and inmate, chauffeur and employer, etc.

• Taking the time for some cuddling.

Christopher and I still find cuddling a very sexually exciting behavior—even with three dogs and a cat in the same bed.

• Having sex in different places or at different times. A few years of having sex on the same mattress in the same bedroom can get boring. You can have sex in other areas of your home, out in the garden, in a motel room, or in the car.

Now that they are retired, Jeff and Gary have decided they don't have to have sex just in the evening. After breakfast, they go back to bed and have a "busy" morning.

• Give each other a body massage.
• Look at each other and say erotic things.
• Have a sexually open relationship (but be aware that this behavior can create other problems for many male couples).
• Watch pornographic videotapes or DVDs.
• Create sexual fantasies in which you engage in sexual behaviors you have never done but have always wanted to try. While having sex with your lover, for example, create a sexual fantasy about having sex with another man who is not your lover. Your fantasies may also involve forced sexual encounters, sex with more than one person, sex in romantic places, and sex in places you've only read about. Fantasies can add excitement to relationships.
• Tell each other the sexual fantasies you have created. Then each of you should try to meet as many of these fantasies as possible.

Activity
Both you and your lover write a sexual fantasy on a piece of paper. The fantasy can involve any person or any activity. Then exchange your fantasy with each other. Talk about them and make some changes so they are exciting to both of you. Then try them out.

6. BE ROMANTIC
Don't forget the romance. Even after umpteen years together it is still nice to celebrate Valentine's Day with a candlelit dinner

and music. Romance is the special part of our relationship that focuses on just the two of us. Sex is exciting, but it's romance that puts the passion into our relationship and makes "our hearts skip a beat."

Activity

Have a date with each other—go out to dinner, go dancing, become romantic, and then go home early (without too much alcohol) and have sex.

7. DO NOT COMPARE YOURSELF WITH SURVEYS THAT REPORT HOW MANY TIMES A WEEK, MONTH, OR YEAR GAY MEN SUPPOSEDLY HAVE SEX OR HOW OFTEN THE "AVERAGE" MALE COUPLE HAS SEX

There is a problem with surveys or listening to other men about their sex lives; we begin to compare our sex lives with theirs and we can never measure up. We then begin to believe there is something wrong with us, blame our lover, or try to change our expectations to match the men in the surveys. The problem with surveys is that men tend to brag a lot about sex and most bragging is really about men lying.

Men in successful relationships (my survey) are still sexually active with each other and they report that sex gets better over the years. The only "given" is that both of the men will also continue to grow older as their relationship continues and becomes long lasting.

In spite of all the myths and rumors you have heard, aging does not necessary cause problems in our relationships. For some male couples, however, one or both men may have difficulty getting an erection, having an orgasm, or lose their interest in having sex. An important **lesson** for all men is that having sex does not mean you always have to have an erection or an orgasm, as shocking as that may sound. For example, touching can be a very sexually exciting behavior.

Activity

Spend an hour with your lover experiencing a full body massage. Each of you gets 30 minutes to be massaged. You massage him for 30 minutes and he massages you for 30 minutes. Use the bed or the floor (using sheets on the floor). Use oil designed for a massage (or any body lotion).

While being massaged, communicate what feels good and what doesn't feel good. You are to be selfish and just enjoy being massaged. He rubs you everywhere following your directions—massaging where you tell him it feels good and when to stop massaging in other places. He is to please you. You may even find being massaged sexually exciting. Even if he doesn't enjoy massaging you, he is to please you for 30 minutes. Then change places and you are to massage him.

After the hour of massaging, talk with each other. How did this feel? What felt good? What would you like to do again? Was it sexually exciting?

SEXUAL ISSUES THAT CAN CAUSE PROBLEMS FOR MALE COUPLES

MONOGAMY OR A SEXUALLY OPEN RELATIONSHIP

I don't know how many male couples are monogamous, but I have learned from talking with many men that the number of monogamous couples has increased during recent decades. I have also learned that **both monogamy and a sexually open relationship can work, but most successful couples have chosen to be monogamous.**

Choosing to be in a monogamous relationship, however, requires a lot of work to keep it sexually exciting. But having a sexually open relationship also requires work—the two of you must develop and maintain a "sexually open relationship agreement." **Men in successful relationships who have a sexually open relationship have an agreement about their sexual behavior outside the relationship.** This agreement, however, has to be:

• what you both want
• one you both can live with

• mutually agreed on
• voluntary

An agreement to have a sexually open relationship (or monogamy) will not be successful if either one of you feels blackmailed into agreeing to something that he doesn't really want.

Bill and Tony have been in love and a couple for two years. Bill describes himself as married to Tony, but not in a monogamous relationship. Monogamy doesn't feel comfortable to him; he has needs that are not met in a monogamous relationship with Tony. Tony is not comfortable with a sexually open relationship but he knows that Bill will leave if he doesn't agree.

Tony met a man one night and had sex with him. But when they started going out to dinner once a week, Bill got angry. Having sex with other men was acceptable; however, having dinner with these men was not. Bill and Tony soon separated.

Both men must also agree to guidelines for a sexually open relationship. Shall the lovers describe the outside sexual relationships to each other? Is it acceptable for each lover to have sex with others only during separate vacations or when apart? Can they have sex with another only one night a week? Can they have sex with someone else in their home? In their bed? Are only three-ways permissible? A "typical" agreement to have a sexually open relationship might include:

• I will only engage in safer-sex behaviors.
• I will come home every night.
• I will not have sex with anyone else in our bed.
• I will not have sex with anyone else in our home.
• I will tell you about it.
• I must obtain your approval each time I have sex outside of our relationship.

• I will have sex outside of our relationship only if you are also included.
• I will not get involved with anyone I have sex with, such as going out on a date, having dinner with him, going to a movie, etc.
• I will only engage in the following sexual behaviors:
  • oral sex
  • masturbation
  • kissing
  • caressing

CHEATING

Contrary to what most gay men believe, not all men cheat on their lover. Cheating is not the same as having a sexually open relationship—it's secretive.

Cheating involves one of the men in a relationship having sex with another man and not telling his lover, probably even lying about it. In my experience, cheating often spells the end of the relationship, not because of the affair but because of the loss of trust that occurs as a result of the dishonesty.

An affair becomes known (and most affairs do eventually become known) because:

• one of the men will confess to having an affair
• a "dear friend" will do all the talking
• there are indications—the lover having the affair will work longer hours, spend more time shopping or at the gym, and may receive secretive phone calls

However, relationships do survive, even though learning your lover is having an affair can be devastating. Even if the relationship survives, putting it back together is a long-term, difficult task for many male couples. Here are some suggestions that may help.

FOR THE LOVER WHO HAD THE AFFAIR:
• Make sure your intention in confessing to your lover is to

improve your relationship and not simply to ease your feeling of guilt or to try to hurt him.

• Do not confess when you are having a fight, you are angry, or when you have been drinking.

• When you tell him or when he finds out about the affair, assure him you still love him (assuming you do still love him and want your relationship with him to continue).

• Keep communication going between the two of you. If he doesn't want to talk now, make sure you continue the discussion again soon. Even if it takes hours, do not become silent.

FOR THE LOVER WHO HAS LEARNED ABOUT THE AFFAIR:
Confront your lover with your suspicions even if you're afraid of the answer. State firmly, "I think you are having an affair."

• Do not ask a question—"Are you having an affair?"

• Don't give conflicting messages—"If you are having an affair, I don't want to know," or "If I ever find out, I'll leave."

• You need to find out what is really going on. Go back and review all the previous chapters in this book.

JEALOUSY

Remember when you were feeling jealous because your lover was cruising a cute guy at a party? You heard he was having lunch every day with a new guy at work? When a friend tried to seduce him? There are very few men who haven't felt jealous sometime during their relationship.

Many of us believe that feeling jealous is wrong. You may try to hide your jealous feelings, you may even agree to have a sexually open relationship because you believe you shouldn't be feeling this way. But we all feel jealous, and it doesn't have to be viewed negatively. Jealousy is neither proof of love (as some men believe), nor proof of emotional immaturity (as other men believe). Jealousy is best dealt with by recognizing it and discussing it when it happens. After all, it's "normal" to feel jealous when you see your lover drooling over some stud at the gym, or when you see him enjoying being cruised by some gorgeous guy at a bar. But it's not OK for you to act on your jealousy, such as when you:

- question him for being late
- monitor his phone calls
- follow him when he goes out alone
- read his mail
- demand to know where he is at all times
- get angry, have arguments and fights just because he looks at another guy or leaves your side when you're both out
- lie awake at nights worrying about the situation and reviewing the evidence: *Was he really cruising him? I wonder if he has made plans to meet him? Is he attracted to him? I wonder if all our friends know about it.*
- get drunk or high to forget the feelings
- threaten violence or suicide
- frantically beg him to stop doing whatever he is doing
- have an affair to get even

Since there is always the potential for jealousy in our relationships, what can you do about it? I recommend being honest and to using "I" statements. Tell him what is going on with you. For example, rather than attacking your lover for flirting with a very attractive man at a party, you can say: "I felt anxious as I watched you with Justin. There were butterflies in my stomach and I started to imagine you were making plans to see him later. I got scared." Such a response, which shares something about you and why you were feeling jealous, allows your lover to respond empathetically to your hurt and fears. Honesty is the best way to handle jealousy.

GROWING OLDER
While I was teaching, I frequently asked my undergraduate students who were 18 to 20 years old at what age sex stops for men. Many of the men answered (and I'm not kidding) "around 40." The truth is that there is no age limit for having sex for physically healthy men.

While Christopher and I were visiting Jeff and Gary for their 50th anniversary celebration, Jeff and I had some time set aside so he could speak privately with me. He was concerned that Gary never initiated sex anymore and appeared no longer to be interested in it. In fact, they hadn't had sex for about two months. They had always enjoyed watching porn together and even this had also stopped. Jeff had discussed his concerns with Gary, who then agreed to have a medical examination, but his physician found nothing physically wrong to explain this change in his sexual behavior.

After 50 years with the man whom he continued to love, Jeff was feeling disappointed in their sex life (as well as feeling horny) and was worried about Gary. I told Jeff that some men do lose their interest in having sex and some even stop having sex as they get older, but that there were still many men in their 80s who continued having great sex lives. I agreed to talk with Gary before Christopher and I left California.

Gary told me he was having trouble getting an erection while having oral sex with Jeff. He believed that because of his age this was "normal," and he now felt "sexually old." He didn't want to keep trying to get an erection, so he stopped having sex. I told Gary the major changes that occur with aging are that the penis (1) takes longer to get erect and (2) needs more physical stimulation in order to get erect. And because of these changes, he probably would not get an erection solely through oral sex. I recommended that (1) Jeff spend more time "playing" with Gary's penis before having oral sex, (2) they do the massage activity, (3) they engage in mutual masturbation, and (4) he call me after I returned to Florida to let me know what happened.

Jeff and Gary called me a few weeks later to let me know they were masturbating together while watching porn.

Men in successful relationships realize that great sex is about sharing with each other, being nurturing, communicating likes and dislikes, experimenting with new sexual behaviors, and hav-

ing fun together. I think Christopher is the greatest sexual partner even after all these years together.

However, no relationship remains stagnant. Over the years
there are changes in our relationships as we progress through the
four stages of being a male couple.

Chapter Eight
Going Through Stages of Change With Mr. Right

Relationships go through stages of change, and each one presents a unique challenge for the male couple. I first heard about these stages in the early 1980s when doctors David P. McWhirter and Andrew M. Mattison were discussing their work with male couples at a meeting in California (which they later published in their classic book, *The Male Couple*).

I was extremely fascinated by the idea of stages, but at the same time I said to myself, *I don't believe we are that predictable.* But in working with hundreds of male couples during the next 20 years, I also observed that all couples really do go through stages. However, each couple is unique as to:

• when these stages occur
• the intensity of each stage
• the duration of each stage

Furthermore, each couple may move from their present stage to an earlier stage and then back to their present stage. What is important is that no couple can skip any of the stages. **Men in successful relationships do the work involved in each of the stages through which their relationships pass.**

STAGE 1: THE HONEYMOON STAGE

There is a lot of romance and warm feelings for each other when you begin your relationship with Mr. Right. Together, you are happy, content, satisfied, nurtured, cared for, and well loved. This is the time when you have an insatiable desire for one another—you may even have sex on the kitchen floor while your dinner burns. You discover how many ways you are similar, more than you even thought possible. Everything is so romantic; you don't care about anything else except just being together. You are very happy and excited. Your relationship is everything you want it to be. Life is so perfect.

This is the honeymoon stage. This stage is a time of satisfaction for both of you. It is the time when you believe all of your expectations for the relationship will be met and nothing will ever go wrong. No problem is insurmountable. Nothing will ever get between the two of you (well, almost nothing).

It is also the time when you see him the way you want to see him. When he does do things you don't like, you tend to deny them or at least believe they are unimportant. You each think the other's weirdness is cute rather than annoying. You focus on similarities and do things to please each other. You do anything to get along. You tend to go above and beyond all of his expectations. He does the same. You do things for each other in order to show your love.

At times you may get a little grumpy with each other and you have little quarrels every now and then but these are minor irritations and they just make it more fun to kiss, have sex, and make up. Regardless of what other people think and tell you, your expectation is that this relationship will last forever. All of our relationships begin with this stage. I believe the honeymoon stage is perhaps the most important stage of all because it:

- lets the two men, who still don't know each other that well, get to know each other
- provides each man with a lot of wonderful memories and a source of satisfaction for the years ahead
- builds the foundation for a successful relationship

But even though everything is perfect, there is still work to be done. **During the honeymoon stage you must be honest about your expectations: These expectations form the foundation of your relationship as a male couple.** During the time between having sex on the kitchen floor and looking into each other's eyes and expressing your undying love, you should be talking about your expectations from each other and from the relationship.

However, because this stage feels so good—we are so happy and so "in love"—many men don't do this work. Therefore, many men begin their relationship with expectations that are false:

- Their lover will fill some void in their life, raise their self-esteem or self-worth, bring them the happiness that has eluded them, end their loneliness, or heal some childhood abuses.
- Our vision for the future is identical. For example, we will share all expenses, we will be monogamous, the holidays will be spent together, and our future home will be in the suburbs with two dogs and a rose garden.

These false and unshared expectations create problems later in the relationship. That's why I recommended in Chapter Four that you see a qualified relationship therapist during the honeymoon stage. This therapist will help you to identify and verbalize your expectations, understand and accept your lover's expectations, resolve the problems that these expectations may present, consider the consequences of both of your expectations, see if there are any alternative expectations, and develop reasonable expectations for the future. The work during this stage is to identify your relationship contract.

Stage 2: The Disappointment Stage

We present the best picture of ourselves during the honeymoon stage. We tell each other what we want to hear. We do what we can to please each other. We see each other the way we want to and neither one of us sees anything wrong with the other. Then *wham*, everything starts to go wrong. Let's again review a few excerpts from the e-mail messages I received after *Mr. Right Is Out There* was published:

• "The first six months of our relationship were wonderful, but now he is gradually beginning to pull away from me."
• "I just finished reading your book *Mr. Right Is Out There*, and thoroughly enjoyed it. I had been in a relationship for three years that recently ended. We love each other—we still do. But all we did was argue. The constant fighting got to both of us."
• "I love him so much. We dated for six months and lived together for three and a half years. I love spending time with him. He's funny, he's good looking, he's smart, and he makes me laugh. I can't imagine my life without him. He is my first real boyfriend. I want to be with him always, but we keep arguing over and over. We are both tired of these fights."

Since these men didn't do the work of the honeymoon stage, they found themselves disappointed in their relationship and in each other after a period of bliss. Then the disagreements and the arguments began. Remember, however, no couple can skip any of these stages. So as much as I hate to say it, we all have to go through the disappointment stage—but our relationship does not have to end during this stage.

That romanticized picture you had of each other begins to crumble during the disappointment stage. You see his faults and he sees yours. You find yourself saying, "I can't believe I didn't see this before. How could I have fallen in love with this guy?" You start to wonder if you made a wrong choice in a lover—once again. You ask, "What has happened to him (us)?"

He told you he hated dogs and didn't want any pets, but you really believed his love for you would send him to the pet store to buy you a dog for your very first Christmas together. However, he didn't buy a dog and continued to hate dogs. After a couple of years, you went out and bought a dog, and the arguments began.

There's a tendency to hurt each other. Sometimes it feels as if you are walking on eggshells. Little things that seem so unimportant turn into big things. Winning an argument and being right becomes more important than the relationship. The following behaviors tell you that you are now in the second stage of your relationship—a time of disappointment.

- You really get irritated when he leaves the cap off the toothpaste, or squeezes it in the middle, or rolls the toilet paper the "wrong" way.
- You have your first real fight. This fight is different from your previous arguments because you try to hurt each other. All of the little things you've learned about him become weapons. You now go for his jugular vein.
- You believe that the relationship would be better if he were different.
- You talk to a friend more than you do to him, especially about being unhappy.
- You hear the door slam shut and he doesn't take the time to kiss you goodbye.
- You think something like, *I don't know what I ever saw in this asshole.*
- You both stop sharing your hopes and dreams with each other.
- He stops:
  - leaving you "love" notes
  - bringing you little gifts
  - calling you from work to tell you he loves you
  - bringing you breakfast in bed

• kissing you during and after sex
• Both of you use "you" statements to blame each other for everything that goes wrong.
  • "It's your fault! If you just weren't _____ ."
  • "If you would just _____ then everything would be great."
  • "Why can't you get it right?"
• You stop laughing together.
• Both of you stop remembering the good times you had together during the honeymoon stage.
• You stop doing things together and avoid each other by sleeping, working, drinking, playing sports, going out with friends, etc.

Anger and resentment starts to build and the downward spiral begins. One of the biggest problems for male couples is that we didn't know the disappointment stage existed. Nobody warned us that:

• we could wake up one morning and regret being in a relationship
• we might become vicious during that first fight
• we would be feeling a lot of hurt and anger about Mr. Right
• feeling disappointed in the relationship is a "normal" stage for all couples

Then our well-meaning friends—during this stage when we need all the support we can get—make comments like, "You deserve better" or "I never really liked him." They may even introduce you to the "new guy in town." These friends remind you that gay relationships never last (a homophobic message).

Because of all the disappointments, as well as the hurt, anger, and lack of support, many male couples decide to end their relationship. **That's why the average relationship for male couples never lasts through the disappointment stage.** But it doesn't have to be that way.

During the honeymoon stage it was: "It's so cute how he always leaves his underwear on the floor" or "I love the way he cuddles with me while he sleeps." But at some point in the relationship those cute things he did during the honeymoon stage aren't so cute anymore. Then one or both of you asserts your own expectations, and it becomes:

• "Why can't you (I **expect** you to) put your underwear in the laundry basket?"
• "I need more room in the bed, you keep sleeping on my side (I **expect** a good night's sleep, so leave me alone)."

As soon as these conflicts in the relationship begin, one or both of you has to acknowledge the situation and begin the process of negotiating your different expectations. This negotiation is a part of being a male couple. **During the "disappointment stage" you negotiate your different expectations.** However, this process will become easier if you both realize you still have love for each other, even if you are fighting. If you lacked feelings for each other, you wouldn't be fighting. Fighting means you still care enough for each other to invest the time and energy into fighting.

Jeff and Gary talked about some of the problems they have had in their relationship over the past 50 years. They each lived with their parents after getting out of the Navy; however, when they started living together they argued repeatedly about Jeff's friends. They both recalled vividly the "big argument that almost ended their relationship."

They were leaving for a movie one night when a friend of Jeff's called. The conversation was about the friend's most recent boyfriend. Gary kept pointing to his watch, mouthing the words, "It's time to go. We're going to be late!" Jeff looked away, thinking, "It would be rude to hang up when my friend is so upset about his new boyfriend having an affair."

Jeff finally got off the phone, but they didn't go to the movie. Instead, they argued about Jeff putting his friends before Gary's need (expectation) for more time together. In Jeff's way of thinking, their argument was about his need (expectation) to spend more time with his friends. Jeff and Gary were no different from many other male couples who frequently argue about friends, family, or former lovers during this stage. The arguments are about their different expectations.

Gary and Jeff wanted to stay in the relationship, and they did the work of negotiating their different expectations. Fifty years together was the outcome of their work.

Negotiating obviously requires that both men have learned how to be Mr. Right (review Chapter Two)—they talk, listen, ask questions, clarify responses, respond with empathy, and repeat what each other has said back to see if they understand the meaning.

- "I really miss getting flowers from you like I use to."
- "I hadn't realized that. What is it you miss about getting flowers?"
- "When I use to get flowers from you, I knew how important I was to you."
- "I'm glad you told me. I was just trying to stay within our budget because now that we are living together I really didn't think we could afford flowers like when we were single."

That may sound like a difficult process, but it allows you **to clarify your expectations in concrete terms**. In other words, your expectations should be stated as behaviors. Men tend to think concretely. For example:

- "I wish you would tell me you love me."
- "What do you mean? I'm working extra hours to make enough money so that I can afford our trip to Paris. Doesn't that let you know I love you?"
- "Well, I need to hear it sometimes."
- "Why do you need to hear it? I show my love to you every day."

Usually all that is needed are small behavioral changes in one or both men, such as more attentiveness, more compliments, more affection, and less complaining.

Most of the male couples who reach this stage do want to stay together. They work diligently to improve their relationships and to negotiate their different expectations. But you must first identify the different expectation causing these problems, then negotiate change (review the guidelines for requesting changes in Chapter Three). You have an easier time negotiating changes, however, if you have identified your expectations earlier in the relationship.

Getting through the disappointment stage and becoming a successful male couple is possible for you if you are both willing to do the work. It never just happens by itself. Don't throw away your relationship because it feels uncomfortable or the work looks difficult. You will most likely only repeat the same disappointments in the next relationship. The most important thing to know is that this stage is a prerequisite to moving to the next stage of relating to each other as couple.

STAGE 3: THE COUPLE STAGE

One day you realize he's stopped complaining about your dirty socks on the bedroom floor. You also realize he's still squeezing the toothpaste in the middle, but it doesn't seem to bother you anymore—and even more, you've stopped nagging him about it. You've now arrived at the Couple Stage of your relationship—you have chosen to be a couple even though you know the good and bad of each other.

Even though you have identified yourself as a couple for some time, it is during this stage that there is a heightened sense of belonging with each other. During this stage, you both:

• accept that this is who you each are and that neither one of you will ever change
• respect one another as separate and unique individuals
• give up believing that the other's expectations are the source of all the problems in the relationship

This stage is enjoyable and rewarding because you both finally accept each other and acknowledge that you really like each other (you talk about loving each other in the previous stages, but in this stage you both also realize you like each other). The two of you talk freely about things that are important to you. You are able to take a position on issues, which may be different from your lover's position, and not feel threatened by so doing. You participate in mutual self-disclosure, sharing your innermost thoughts and feelings, and tell things about yourself that you may not have shared with anyone else. You can say anything and know his response will be totally accepting. You know the strengths of each other, as well as the weaknesses. You also nurture each other during illness, difficulty, hardship, and crisis. Each of you is connected to the other and really cares about the other's well-being. During this stage, you are truly best friends.

In the couple stage, you (1) develop your shared expectations in order to (2) define your own identity as a male couple. Either you learn to do this work together or you go back to the second stage and continue to do the work of accepting your different expectations. There may be disagreements in doing this work, but the disagreements are not about your different expectations in this stage. These disagreements are about your shared expectations in order to define your own identity as a male couple. This identity may be different from your respective families, from nongay couples, and from other male couples.

In Chapter Six, Al talked about his dream (expectation) of always having children. Lance was able to verbalize that he didn't want to have children. Two years later, they celebrated their 12th anniversary along with Al being an elementary school teacher. However—prior to completing the manuscript for this book, I received an e-mail message from Al saying that Lance had changed his mind about having children and they had just gotten back from South America where they adopted a boy. The message said they were both very happy.

For our first few years as a couple, Christopher and I would spend Thanksgiving in Bermuda. We loved the culture, the warm weather, getting away from Philadelphia—but the real truth is that we had not yet clarified for ourselves how we wanted to spend our Thanksgiving as a couple. Our respective families had their expectations for us—we would have a traditional Thanksgiving at their homes. But whose home—with my mother in California or with Christopher's mother in Pennsylvania? Friends expected us to be with them, but which friends? The potential conflicts were avoided by going to Bermuda.

We had to do the work to identify what we wanted (our expectations) for our own Thanksgiving. Once we did that, we stopped going to Bermuda and started spending Thanksgiving with "our family." We still do—in Florida we now have Thanksgiving at home with our own four "children"—Alexa the cat, Kahli the dachshund, Fauna the Yorkie, and Marriquita the Chihuahua. Also included in our Thanksgiving is "our family."

Defining "family" is important work during this stage. So many gay men don't do this work and continue to define their family as their blood relatives.

Even though Jeff and Gary are both 75 years old, have been a couple for 50 years, are both now retired, and have many friends, Thanksgiving and Christmas are celebrated by inviting their respective families to a festive dinner. Family for Jeff and Gary consists of their siblings and their nieces and nephews. Even though Jeff and Gary are a successful couple, their homophobia prevents them from including their many gay and nongay friends in these holiday dinners.

Men in successful relationships have a "family," which usually includes their relatives, as well as those friends (gay and nongay) who love, support, and respect them as a couple.

In our Thanksgiving, Christopher and I include "our family," our neighbors George and Louis (a male couple), Nancy and Robert (a nongay couple), Marylyn and Ed (Christopher's mother and stepfather), and our "four children" (my mother had been included, but she died last year).

The work in this stage of developing your shared expectations in order to define your own identity as a male couple builds the relationship for the next stage—the successful male couple.

STAGE 4: THE SUCCESSFUL STAGE

In the Introduction to *Mr. Right Is Out There*, I identified 33 male couples who were our friends. Of these couples, I know that 21 continue to be successful male couples; four are no longer couples because one or both of the men have died; we have lost contact with three couples; and five couples became unsuccessful. I know our friends may not be a representative sample of male couples, but five unsuccessful couples out of 33 doesn't support the homophobic myth that relationships between two men are rarely successful.

The successful stage seems to begin rather suddenly, even though you have been a couple for quite some time and you have been through a lot together. One day you realize the two of you haven't had a disagreement for a long time. In fact, you can't even remember the last time you had an argument. Most couples are surprised at how relaxed their time together has now become. At this stage, there is the knowledge the two of you have chosen to be with each other. You make decisions knowing:

• whom each of you is
• your individual expectations
• your shared expectations

You look at him and know he is your best friend, you are glad you are in a relationship with him, and you are looking forward to many more years of togetherness: You are now at the successful stage.

George and Louis are our neighbors in Florida. They are the only long-term couple I have ever known who met each other as teenagers; they will soon be celebrating their 25 anniversary. George and Louis are best friends, and they truly are in the successful stage of their relationship.

Does this mean there are no problems in this stage? Of course not! The major problem, however, comes about because you both feel very secure as a couple—it really does feel like the two of you will be together "till death do you part." Since you aren't spending so much time and energy on those couple disagreements and arguments of the previous three stages, you now have more time to explore those individual interests that have been neglected. Too many couples in this stage, however, let the time slip away with their individual interests, and the couple gets neglected because of it.

Jeff and Gary's commitment to each other is secure; however, like many other long-term couples, they spend less and less time with each other. Since they are now both retired, Gary devotes much of his free time to the local horticulture society where he has recently been elected vice president. He also enters many of his roses into competition. Jeff has always been interested in cooking and has started taking classes. He spends his free time creating new recipes with his fellow classmates.

Since the couple may now be spending more time on their individual interests and less time on couple interests, **the work for you to do in the "successful stage" is to nurture your relationship**. There needs to be time for the couple as well as the individual. The couple needs to set aside time to be together to talk about those things friends talk about—interests, dreams, and current events—as well as to be romantic with each other. The couple still needs to take the time to "have a date with each other."

Jeff and Gary have started to make time for talking over a second cup of coffee in the morning (or going back to bed together for "cuddle time"). They are also now taking an evening walk together, and they schedule one day a week for a date with each other—a movie, dinner at a restaurant, or just a walk on the beach.

Another problem in this stage is the "midlife crisis." You've all heard about them, and all of us have or will have them. Somewhere along the way, while sitting at home with your lover, you realize "I'm turning into my parents": You're watching television and taking out the garbage twice a week. It begins to hit:

• You have never been included on that "A list" of gay men who are invited to all those fabulous parties on Fire Island.
• You have just become 30 (or 40, 50, etc.) and all of your friends keep telling you that once you're 30 (or 40 or 50), it's downhill from then on. Then one day it really sinks in—you look in the mirror and you don't look 18 (or 30, 40, or 50) anymore.
• You hate living in Des Moines; you've always wanted to live in San Francisco.
• You are driving a Chevrolet; you've always wanted a Jaguar.
• You are no longer the center of attention at all those parties.
• You have been in a relationship with the same man for 25 years and you start thinking, *Who is this 'old' man I'm living with?* and you begin fantasizing about the 20-year-old "kid" who just started working in your office.

You start thinking, *I better do something about that* (your expectations) *right now before it's too late.*

The midlife crisis is a time in which we review and evaluate what we have done with our life and what we expect out of it. We ask ourselves, *Is this what I want to be doing for the rest of my life?* But for gay men, the name is wrong. Like nongay men, we do have a crisis, but it doesn't always happen in midlife (whatever age that is). Some of us have a midlife crisis in our 20s and 30s. Some of us even have two or three midlife crises. However, there's always a midlife crisis during the successful stage of our relationship.

So what can you do about your midlife crisis? First of all, realize that it's just part of growing older. So if you find your lover going through a change, or if you're experiencing one yourself, try to understand this is "normal." The truth is that your midlife crisis will go away on its own if you just do nothing and wait long enough. You will adjust; you'll get over it. But of course, that's not the answer you wanted.

The best treatment for a midlife crisis is to **change your expectations**.

As you have read earlier in this book, you are in charge of your brain and what you think. As you evaluate your expectations, it's time to realize that:

• Neither Toby Maguire nor Ashton Kutcher is ever going to want to have sex with you. Never! It's an unachievable dream.
• The parties on Fire Island are very superficial.
• A Jaguar may be a great car, but even if you could afford one it doesn't make sense to spend all that money when you hope to retire in 20 years.
• Circuit parties aren't really that exciting, and in fact, you don't really want to go.
• Having a nose job, face-lift, or a little nip and tuck may make you feel better, but it isn't going to change the fact that you still aren't going to be invited to all those "A-list" parties you've heard about.
• Having an affair with the 20-year-old kid at the office may help you to feel better, but only for a while.

Make some changes in your life as you change your expectations. A drastic change could mess up your life, including your relationship. But you can still make some changes—not earth shaking changes, but changes nonetheless.

• If you are not satisfied with what you have accomplished, perhaps it's time to go back to school—take part-time classes, take evening classes, look for scholarship aid.

• Explore changes in your home with your lover, sexual behaviors with each other, getting a pet, moving to a new home, etc.

• Talk with your employer about other options.

• Take the vacation you've always wanted to take.

• Go to San Francisco with your lover. Explore the city. Look for jobs. Check out apartments or the cost of buying a home. Talk to other gay men about the reality of living in San Francisco. How does it compare with Des Moines?

Successful couples are no longer the same as they were during the honeymoon stage. Many of the familiar expectations and behaviors are gone. But change is necessary in order to become a successful male couple.

And We Lived Happily Ever After

In Chapter One, I discussed the e-mail messages I started receiving after the publication of *Mr. Right Is Out There*. Many of these men told me about their successful relationships. For example:

• "I had to write to you to congratulate you on an excellent book. It took me just a few days to read the whole book from start to finish, but I found your book to be totally inspiring. I wanted to tell you about my relationship. I'm a 45-year-old black gay man who has found and maintained a loving and meaningful relationship with the same man for 20 years.

"Our families didn't know at first, but now they do. That has been really great. It feels so supportive. But the big event in our life happened two years ago: We now have twin daughters. Their biological mother is my lover's sister and I'm their biological father, which gives our daughters both our blood. And again, our families were supportive, but not all of our friends. They thought we had made a mistake, but they now see how happy we are and what great fathers we are.

"It's great knowing there are other couples out there—there are not too many where we live. But we are here."

• "I really enjoyed your book; it was fast-paced and easy to read. It has helped me in so many ways and has really made my lover and me think about the things we are now doing in our relationship. The activities and assignments were really cool because it actually gave us the opportunity to experience the things you were talking about.

"We have been together for 8½ years, and I think that at first we didn't do some of the basic things you mentioned in your book. But then one day we just sort of knew we were friends. We stopped arguing because that took the fun out of being together. We started doing the things we did when we were dating. I love this man and I think we will be together forever.

"I really liked your story about your commitment ceremony. I have never really heard the details about a commitment ceremony before, and we are now planning on having one next spring and hope you and Christopher will be able to attend (we live in London)."

• "I just finished reading *Mr. Right Is Out There*; what a terrific book! It's much more down-to-earth and accessible than most. I'm a 55-year-old gay man, and my lover is 57. We live in Idaho and have been together for 18 years. We both admire each other and like each other. He has taught me to be myself and to be a proud gay man. When we met I was closeted and very homophobic; I had been married and have two children.

"We are going to retire in 10 years and plan to travel for a while before moving to New Orleans. That has been our dream since the day we met. By the way, we met at the baths in San Francisco, so some relationships that begin in the baths do make it. He lived in San Francisco, but after a year of phone calls and bus trips he decided to move to Idaho.

"We both like your description of male couples being best friends—that's us. Thanks!"

• "Just a short note to let you know how much I'm enjoying your book. I'm loving every minute of what you have written. I lost my first lover to AIDS, but I had my pictures and my memories. Then four years after he died I met this wonderful man and started dating, but the guilt was so strong that I felt awful and I felt unfaithful. Then one night he held me and took the pictures and suggested I burn them and get on with my life. I was angry, and I stopped seeing him for a month. But I knew he was right. I called him and we went to the ocean and buried the pictures in the sand. We sat together and watched the sun go down. It was very symbolic. That was 10 years ago, and we are still together."

• "I'm 47 and live in Peru. For 13 years I've shared a place here with a man I love. We can never go out as a couple for safety reasons, but we went to New York for a business trip and did all the gay things. We also bought your book. It made us feel good to read about other couples. We may not be like you are in the States, but we are in love, and as you say, we are best friends. You are very inspiring and we would love to correspond with you."

• "My lover of 67 years died last year. I'm 90; he would have been 91. He was cremated, and I have his remains so that mine can be put with his. We will be buried just as we spent our life—together."

As Christopher and I talked about growing older together and eventually dying, we decided to see a lawyer about our wills. In our wills, our "gay-friendly lawyer" used the following words to describe our relationship:

- friends
- object of my affection
- object of my bounty
- significant other
- domestic partner

And after we rejected each newly revised will, he finally wrote an acceptable will that we each signed:

"I give and devise to my **life partner**, Kenneth D. George, with whom I have happily shared my life…"

"I give and devise to my **life partner**, Christopher S. Beck, with whom I have happily shared my life…"

"And they lived happily ever after."